IMPACT FIRST

IMPACT FIRST

THE SOCIAL ENTREPRENEUR'S GUIDE TO MEASURING, MANAGING AND GROWING YOUR IMPACT

HEIDI L. FISHER MBE

First published December 2020.

Printed in the United Kingdom.

ISBN 978-0-9957486-4-4

Every action we take impacts the lives of others around us.

The Question is: Are you aware of Your impact?

Arthur Carmazzi

This book is dedicated to my children, Lewis and Elisha. You inspire me to try to leave the world better than I found it. Never stop being happy.

CONTENTS

ACKNOWLEDGEMENTS

I am grateful to everyone who has been a part of my journey in creating this book. You know who you are! Special thanks to my family for supporting me and encouraging me to write even on the days that I did not feel like it.

Thank you to all of the organisations I have worked with over the years – for your trust and belief in me, which has enabled me to share what I know in this book.

INTRODUCTION

Every social entrepreneur sets out with the vision to create a social or environmental impact – but not every social entrepreneur knows if they are actually making an impact or not.

It makes no sense to do good and not know if it really makes a difference or not. Do not be one of those leaders that assumes you are making a difference – be 100% certain by measuring your impact. Do not be the person who thinks it is ok if you achieve positive impact for 60% of customers. Be the one who asks about the other 40% and manages your impact to move closer to 100% positive impact.

This book takes you through Impact Measurement and Management (IMM). It is a guide, but it is also a way to make it all less complicated, time consuming and confusing. Follow the guidance and you will know what impact you are having and how you can continue to maximise your impact.

It is also more than a guide because I very much hope that you'll recognise the importance of impact measurement and management beyond just understanding your impact on people or the planet – and you will see how it contributes to strategic decisions, business planning, HR, marketing and much more.

We are now at a pivotal point in history where impact measurement and management are becoming increasingly important. The choice is clear – carry on as before or change. Impact first businesses and social enterprises are the change that is needed to ensure there is a world for future generations – a world that cares about the impact it has on people and the planet.

GUIDE TO THIS BOOK

Section One: The Foundations

This Section covers the foundations of impact measurement and management. With all the terminology and underlying principles explained, as well as an introduction to the Lean Social Impact Approach, and the three cross cutting themes (Impact Led Strategy, Communicating Impact and Embedding Impact) including social procurement.

Section Two: Measuring Impact

This Section focuses on the first three stages of the Lean Social Impact Approach (Define, Plan and Measure), and shares different techniques and approaches you can take to measuring your social, community, economic, environmental and technology impact.

Section Three: Managing Impact

This Section details the final two stages of the Approach (Analyse and Learn), as well as Social Return on Investment (SROI). Then moves on to how you can share your impact findings internally and externally, the future of IMM, and how to continue your IMM during times of crisis and change.

Section Four: Further Resources

This Section includes a glossary, all the links (endnotes), and details of the free downloadable resources that I have created to support your IMM processes (available from www.makeanimpactcic.co.uk/impact-first-resources).

Please note beneficiaries is used interchangeably throughout this book with clients, customers and service users. The same applies for activities, which is used interchangeably with product, services and delivery.

I hope you enjoy the book and continue to maximise your impact on people and the planet.

Heidi L. Fisher MBE
December 2020

Section One: The Foundations

CHAPTER 1: BACKGROUND TO IMPACT MEASUREMENT AND MANAGEMENT

It might seem a strange place to start, but for many of you the language around impact measurement and management (IMM) causes a lot of confusion, so to make sure you are clear about exactly what I mean I will be covering some of the key definitions in this Chapter. Crucially you will need to know what your ultimate goal is, what outcomes and impact are, and what measurement and management are. Once you have these things clear then the foundations are in place. You will also learn about the underlying principles for IMM.

DEFINITIONS

Ultimate Goal

The ultimate goal describes the bigger picture problem the organisation is trying to solve and the long-term impact the organisation wants to have, for example, no poverty. Essentially, it is the vision of what the world looks like once you've solved the problem you've set your social enterprise up for, and the changes that you hope will be sustained.

Outcomes

Outcomes are the differences or changes that have occurred with the organisation's stakeholders as a result of the delivery of activities and achievement of outputs – including positive, negative, intended and unintended outcomes. Outcomes tend to be shorter-term changes that lead on to the long-term impact and ultimate goal.

Impact

Impact refers to the proportion of the outcomes the organisation can claim they are responsible for achieving, and refers to social, economic, environmental and community impacts. Impact is the long-term change that is sustained beyond the period of delivery by your organisation.

Social Impact

Social impact is often used to refer to the change that happens to people, the economy, the community and the environment as a result of your activities or services. But strictly speaking social impact is about the changes that happen to people and economic impact, environmental impact and community impact can be defined separately. The changes can be positive, negative, intended or unintended.

Community impact

This is the impact the organisation has on the wider community, for example through community regeneration activities, and includes things that fit within social, economic or environmental impact but affect more than one individual or family. These community impacts affect a whole community, neighbourhood or area.

Economic impact

This is the impact the organisation has on the economy and on the financial resources people have.

Environmental impact

This is the impact the organisation has on the environment.

Social Value

Social value describes the wider social, economic and environmental benefits that derive from an organisation's work or from the commissioning of services or the purchasing of goods. Social value is focused on getting more value from the money you spend. It enables you to maximise the positive impact your work and procurement has on local communities, people and the environment. Social values asks the question, 'If £1 is spent on the delivery of services or the purchasing of goods can that same £1 be used to also produce a wider benefit to the community?'

Impact measurement

Impact measurement is the process of designing systems, consulting with stakeholders, collecting data and measuring the impact you have.

Impact management

Impact management is what your organisation does with the information you have obtained through the impact measurement process to continually improve your organisation so you can increase the level of positive impacts and reduce negative impacts.

Why Are People Talking About Impact Measurement And Management?

Around 2017 people started to talk about IMM rather than just impact measurement. Up until that point everyone focused on measuring their impact and sharing all the positives. But now impact measurement has been renamed as IMM it asks the question, "what about the things that aren't positive and how can you reduce these?"

If you missed this change in terminology don't worry. Pretty much everyone who isn't an impact practitioner hasn't heard the phrase impact management. From your perspective it gives impact measurement a purpose beyond reporting to a funder or investor because they asked for it. It means there is now an equally important emphasis on doing something with the data you get from the measurement stage – so you're actually managing your impact with a view to maximising it (by increasing positive impacts and reducing negative impacts). But more importantly it connects your impact measurement to your business planning and strategic decision making (more on that later).

The Evolution Of IMM

Evaluation has evolved – many funders required evaluations that focused on outputs and evidence that a project or service had been delivered, but this type of evaluation is more focused on the process – has what was planned to be done been done? If not, what could be changed/improved to get things done? It failed to ask the question what difference the service or support had made, and in all honesty, for many organisations, the answer to this question was that it had made little difference. The people who were being supported were often left dependent on that organisation for help. So impact measurement shifted the focus of evaluations to the changes that occurred in peoples' lives, the economy and the environment.

Although impact measurement is relatively new, there are over 170 different methods you can use (please don't read about them all as you'll end up totally confused and overwhelmed, and probably won't do any impact measurement). However, the main two methods are Social Accounting and Audit, and Social Return on Investment.

Social Accounting and Audit is focused on a qualitative approach – engaging stakeholders in assessing how effectively you deliver your values, as well as the outcomes you have achieved, and using case studies and feedback to tell your impact story. The process involves proving, improving and accounting for the difference your organisation makes.

The prove part is focused on gathering evidence of your social, economic and environmental impact (essentially the impact measurement part of the process). Improve is about what you are going to do to improve your performance in the future (the impact management stage). Account is making sure you are accountable to your stakeholders.

The method involves looking at how you have performed in terms of outputs as well as outcomes. The entire process can be quite time consuming but it does enable your organisation to collect data and report it in a way that is relevant and specific to your organisation. Social Accounting and Audit encourages the benchmarking of indicators (for outputs, results and impacts), by using average values from similar organisations, to give some ability to provide comparisons between organisations. The audit stage requires organisations to have their social accounts reviewed, to make sure the data collected is sufficient and valid.

SROI is a method for identifying and valuing the impact a particular service, project or organisation has. Typically it is used where the services are commissioned from the public sector, funded by a grant making body or investor in order to provide a cost-benefit analysis, which is presented as a ratio showing how for every £1 invested £x of social value is produced. SROI can incorporate a number of outcomes including social, economic and environmental outcomes. It can be used to calculate the fiscal savings to government or statutory agencies.

SROI has grown in popularity over the past 15 years, as the NHS and many Social Impact Bonds used the method, but it is not without its critics due to the number of assumptions that are made during the process. Increasingly the financial values assigned to outcomes are being standardised (see Chapter 16), and more soft outcomes have financial values so that SROI can be used by all types of organisations that want to monetise their impact.

As I mentioned there are over 170 different methods for measuring impact – and to go through all of these would take more than a book. You do not need to know about all of these different methods – you really don't - you need to work out a way of measuring and managing impact that makes sense for your organisation.

Personally, I prefer an approach that blends the qualitative data from social accounting with the financial values from SROI, as it gives a more rounded view of what the organisation has achieved, and does not lose the stories and case studies which tell the story in more detail and bring the organisation to life. By having financial values it also satisfies funders or commissioners who might be looking at how this intervention can potentially lead to financial savings.

THE UNDERLYING PRINCIPLES

Underlying IMM are seven principles as defined by Social Value UK. The Social Audit Network (SAN) has a similar set of eight principles.

Social Value Principles

The seven principles[i] used by Social Value UK require you to make judgements and decisions about the most appropriate way to measure your impact. This often makes people fearful that they will make the wrong choice, or do something wrong. In reality, impact measurement is an iterative process where you learn and develop as you go along. If you started by asking just one question, "What difference has our work/support made to your life?" you would get some data. From there you could develop your impact measurement further by making it more focused, more accurate etc. but if you don't start you'll never have any data – and you'll never know what impact you are genuinely having. With that in mind, let's look at each of the seven principles in turn:

Involve stakeholders: Stakeholders are key to your impact measurement and management process, and need to be involved in deciding what gets measured, how it is measured and what values are assigned to the outcomes and impacts.

Understand what changes: It is vital to identify the key changes you create, and to use the impact measurement process to evidence the changes. This includes positive, negative, intended and unintended changes.

Value the things that matter: After identifying the key changes for your different stakeholder groups, the next step is then to give values to these key changes. This is where knowing what matters to your stakeholders is vital, because otherwise you could end up measuring and valuing outcomes that don't matter.

Only include what is material: To ensure your IMM is valid and not too complicated, immaterial items need to be excluded from the process.

Do not over-claim: It is very easy to believe that your organisation is responsible for all the change that has occurred, which would result in you over-claiming the impact you have. This principle is included to make sure you adjust for the proportion of change that other organisations/events are responsible for.

Be transparent: This involves identifying any assumptions used in analysing your impact, and the sensitivity of those assumptions to changes. It also means sharing your findings transparently (the good – your positive impacts, the bad – your negative impacts, and the ugly – the unintended things that happened) is required.

Verify the results: Make sure the results are independently verified or assured to reduce the likelihood of bias.

Social Accounting and Audit Principles

Social Accounting and Audit has eight key principles[ii] that form the basis for the social accounting process:

- Clarify Purpose
- Define Scope
- Engage Stakeholders
- Determine Materiality
- Make Comparisons (benchmarking)
- Be Transparent
- Verify Accounts
- Embed the process – continuous improvement

As you will see, these are very similar to the Social Value Principles, with the exception that there is no requirement to monetise the impact.

How to use these principles

The key thing with these principles is to keep them in mind throughout your impact measurement, reporting and management activities as well as making them part of your organisation's way of doing things. What that actually means is that you know why you are measuring your impact, you are engaging your stakeholders, you have identified who experiences change, what the change is and that the change actually matters to your stakeholders. You are not overstating your impact, and you are being transparent when sharing the findings as well as the areas for improvement. You also know which outcomes and impacts are important enough to manage. We will talk more about these things throughout the book.

Although I will not continually refer to the principles throughout the book, you will need to be making judgements and decisions as to how they influence and affect your IMM processes.

CHAPTER 2: INTRODUCTION TO THE LEAN SOCIAL IMPACT APPROACH

O ver the 15+ years that I've been supporting social enterprises and charities with their IMM, I noticed that a lot of organisations like the idea of IMM, but when they start to read up about it find the whole thing overwhelming and confusing (and usually don't start doing any IMM because it's too much effort and time consuming).

I believe IMM should be manageable, focused and consistent, and that is why I developed the Lean Social Impact Approach – to remove the complexity, enable organisations of any size to implement IMM successfully and to follow the underlying principles in their IMM. I also believe that there needs to be an alternative to the rigours of assurance and audit that focus on verification of what has been measured. Instead, organisations need support to build their confidence in impact measurement and to figure out what managing their impact means for them.

This Chapter will introduce you to the Lean Social Impact Approach before we delve deeper in subsequent Chapters.

THE BASICS OF THE LEAN SOCIAL IMPACT APPROACH

The Lean Social Impact Approach has three cross cutting themes and five stages. The three cross cutting themes interconnect the five stages.

The three cross cutting themes are:

- I - Impact Led Strategy
- C - Communicating impact
- E - Embedding impact

Or ICE. ICE is important to make sure you do not lose sight of the:

- Why
- What
- How
- When

Of your impact measurement and management.

ICE makes sure you are aligned with your overall purpose, measure what matters and use the data to support your organisation's development.

Impact Led Strategy: This is about being led by the impact you want to create and *being* your purpose as an organisation, rather than *having* a purpose.

Communicating Impact: To truly achieve an impact led strategy you need to communicate impact effectively at each stage of the Lean Social Impact Approach.

Embedding Impact: This is about how you make sure your organisation is driven by maximising impact and puts impact at the heart of what you do.

The next four Chapters (Chapters 3-6) focus on these cross cutting themes in more detail.

The five stages are there to provide a step by step process and structure to your IMM that enables you to just get on with it, and I mean 'get on with it', as it takes what you know and what you have already in place and builds from there.

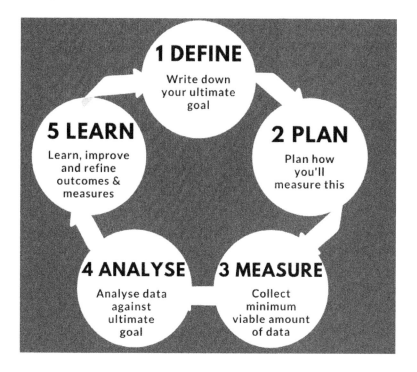

The five stages are:

- Define
- Plan
- Measure
- Analyse
- Learn

Define: This is the first stage of the Lean Social Impact Approach and helps you to get clear about the impact you are trying to create through your organisation's activities.

Plan: My favourite stage – as this is where you get to decide what you will measure and how you will do the measuring. It's also the toughest stage and the one people like to skip over – but investing time here will pay dividends when you move on to stage three (measure).

Measure: This is when you actually get to do the data collection – which if you've planned it properly during stage two will be straightforward.

Analyse: This stage is about taking immediate analysis of the data you are collecting to see what is working and what is not.

Learn: This is the management part of IMM – where you delve deeper in to the data and learn from it as part of your continuous improvement and business planning cycles.

Starting in Chapter 8, we will be working through each of the five stages in more details to develop your IMM.

CHAPTER 3: IMPACT LED STRATEGY

The first cross cutting theme of the Lean Social Impact Approach is Impact Led Strategy. This is about how you approach and view impact as an organisation, and what value you place on your impact data.

Many people fail to see the bigger picture of what IMM can provide for their organisation – don't be one of them. IMM, to me, is one of the most useful and beneficial approaches you can adopt across your organisation – because it will make the following better:

- Decision making
- Strategic focus
- New product and service development and innovation
- Marketing
- How embedded your organisation's values and ultimate goal are
- Your staff and HR

You'll find out more about communicating impact in Chapter 4 and embedding impact in Chapters 5 and 6, as together they are essential for the implementation of an Impact Led strategy, and effective IMM.

WHAT IS AN IMPACT LED STRATEGY?

You may have heard the term impact led (or perhaps you've heard people talking about being value led when referring to social value). It means you are led as an organisation by the impact you want to create, and you're focused on maximising your impact by having a business strategy that has that focus too. Basically it means moving from *having* a social or environmental purpose to *being* your purpose.

Many organisations have become bogged down in a cycle of continuing to exist – which means chasing funding and contracts to continue delivering the same services and keeping their employees in jobs. This approach doesn't always address whether the real mission is being delivered properly, or at all.

Your organisation can become complacent and stop evolving because you never question if the way you deliver your activities is really the best way to achieve change. By focusing on an Impact Led strategy you can review what you do with fresh eyes, and see if every aspect of your organisation is working towards the same goal – from the ethics behind the suppliers you use to the welfare of your staff.

And the biggest reason for bothering with an Impact Led strategy is that if you're really great at what you do and are maximising your impact you can have an ambition to close down because the problem you set out to address is solved.

TAKING A LONG-TERM APPROACH

An Impact Led strategy is not a short-term approach. It's recognising that you may potentially not create any impact for many years (or possibly several generations), rather than delivering a short term intervention that will deliver immediate results. The problem with this is that the results taper off very quickly and there is no lasting impact.

I guess that's why many organisations, when faced with a choice between doing something with immediate outcomes, versus something with long-term sustainable inter-generational change, will pick the former. It's also why the government or the health service don't invest in preventative services – because society want to see progress and change quickly – or they get voted out at the next election – and to appease the electorate short-term intervention type work is funded. The same applies to funders – although I am seeing some progress in this area with funders considering five year and ten year programmes in order to deliver real long-term impact. But I think we are a long way off from this being the norm, because people demand and want immediate crisis intervention.

To implement an Impact Led strategy will most likely require a transition period – as most organisations nowadays deliver short-term intervention, and to shift to also delivering long-term impact will take time. The key to achieving this is to start to strategically shift where your resources are focused (to maximising long-term impact rather than outputs). But the question is, do you have the commitment to invest in something that may not see any results for 10-20 years or more?

How to Develop an Impact Led Strategy

An impact led strategy doesn't just require a focus on maximising impact it also requires you to put creating impact at the heart of your organisation – rather than the delivery of an activity, service or product. This requires your CEO or Board to be committed to this approach in their thinking, and not to switch back to being led by what you have always done.

Usually your organisation will develop its strategy based on what you are currently doing – the services/products you currently deliver and the financial resources you have. This is the typical business planning approach where the current figures get a +5% (or whatever figure is deemed appropriate), and no real thought is given as to whether the products and services are the right ones to achieve impact.

An impact led approach flips most of the traditional business planning and strategy development on its head, and asks how can you create the most impact for the people you work with (or for the environment)?

What does this look like in reality?

The typical business planning process looks like this:

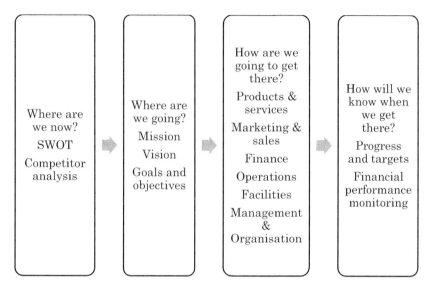

With an impact led strategy it looks like this:

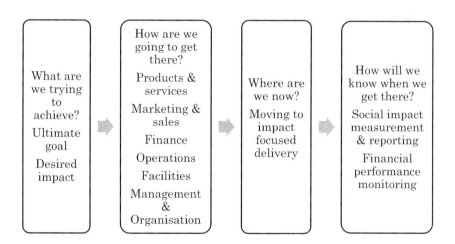

Once you have identified the impact you desire, the next step is to look at how you can best achieve this. To do this you decide which products and services (existing or new ones) will deliver these outcomes and impact for you. Finally, you look at how you can use the existing resources you have to deliver this (or do you need more/less money – or do you need to work with more/less people?), and start to shift from your current strategy to an impact led strategy.

The Steps to creating an Impact Led Strategy
To actually develop an impact led strategy there are a number of steps. This section provides an overview of the first two. You will find out more about the third step in Chapter 5 – Embedding Impact).

1. Decide on the problem you want to solve. What is the desired impact are you trying to have on society or the planet? Examples could include:

   All children are free from cancer

   Everyone has access to safe and affordable accommodation

   People are free from domestic abuse

2. How can you best solve this problem? To answer this question don't focus on what you currently do as this may not be the best way to solve the problem and create the most impact. Ask the following questions:

   If money time and resources were not an issue, what would the ideal product or service look like to achieve this desired impact?

   How, when and where would it be delivered?

   Who would the product or service be delivered to?

If any of those answers differ to your current activities, then there could be a disconnect, and now's a great time to re-evaluate.

WHAT OTHER ASPECTS DO YOU NEED TO CONSIDER?

At every point of the strategy development you need to ask yourself if what you are planning to do will maximise your impact:

- Which activities/services will contribute most to achieving the impact?
- How will you know you are achieving your desired impact?
- How will you measure if you are having the impact you intended?
- Do your performance measures include impact measures as well as financial measures?
- Is this data regularly shared across the organisation and reported to the Board?
- Is impact the focus for learning and development in the organisation?
- Do you focus on how you can continually improve and learn from your delivery to generate more impact?
- Is impact measurement and reporting part of your job descriptions, objectives and appraisals for every employee?

The final question to ask throughout the development of your impact led strategy is: **Does this help to create and achieve a greater impact? If not, why are you doing it?**

This final question is really a sense check – to make sure what you are planning to do is not taking you off track from your long-term purpose and desired impact. It is very easy to react to short-term issues, and shift away, or diverge, from your impact led goal.

Once you are clear about what products and services will maximise impact, you can then start to look at how you can best use your resources to deliver these activities; and also what you need to stop or transition away from doing as it is not achieving your desired impact.

CHAPTER 4: COMMUNICATING IMPACT

C ommunicating impact is the second cross cutting theme. Communication of impact is vital at all levels in your organisation as well as with all your stakeholders. This includes communicating the positive impacts as well as the negative impacts, and what you will do to improve your impact.

WHAT NEEDS COMMUNICATING

You are probably sat there thinking, "communicating impact - that's easy. I'll just talk to a few people." But it's also the theme that gets forgotten which can lead to miscommunication and understandings in the following areas:

- Why are you measuring your impact?
- What are the benefits of measuring your impact?
- Who is responsible and accountable for measuring impact?
- What are you actually measuring, how and for whom?
- What are you doing with the data that's collected?
- How will you know if you've been successful or not?

- How does it affect your continual improvement and the organisation's future plans?
- How will you share the findings from the data?
- Who will you share the findings with?

These questions specifically relate to the five areas of the Lean Social Impact Approach. By integrating effective communication at each of the stages you'll nail this theme! You'll also avoid all the objections at each stage of the process because you will have already pre-empted their questions, such as "Why have we got to get all this extra data?" and "I don't have time to do this." or "I don't see the point in doing this."

Let's talk about how you can integrate effective communication at each stage in the rest of this Chapter.

HOW TO EFFECTIVELY COMMUNICATE IMPACT

Communicating impact in the Define Stage

The key questions here are:

- Why are you measuring your impact?
- What are the benefits of measuring your impact?

These questions are about making sure everyone understands why you're doing it in the first place. Your motivations for measuring your impact are usually triggered by a specific event or need. These could be one of the following (or something else):

- To report back to a funder
- To communicate what you do and your impact

- To make sure you are operating effectively
- To identify where you can make improvements
- To evidence how you comply with the Social Value Act
- To identify the potential savings you make for the public sector
- To monetise your social value and calculate a SROI figure

By being clear about your motivations for measuring your impact you'll be able to explain why you are doing this and increase the likelihood of buy-in from your Board, staff, volunteers, clients and other stakeholders. I'll talk about this again in Chapter 7, as this is important.

The second element here is being clear about the benefits. In most cases there are only two primary reasons for measuring impact:

- To increase your organisation's income
- To increase your organisation's impact

There may be secondary reasons, such as:

- Having the evidence to win a tender, secure a grant or gain investment
- Providing information to develop new products or services
- Helping to develop a better organisational culture
- Improving your marketing

But, ultimately these all contribute to one of the two primary reasons (increasing income or increasing impact).

Communicating impact in the Plan Stage

In the Plan stage you are focusing on what you are going to measure, so it's vitally important to communicate the following clearly:

- Who is responsible and accountable for measuring impact?
- What are you actually measuring, how and for whom?

The key distinction here is that someone will be accountable for making sure impact measurement happens. It may be you or someone senior within your organisation. You will then delegate responsibility for certain tasks and activities, that enable the impact measurement to happen on a day to day basis. (If there's only you in the organisation then you're both accountable and responsible!)

Communicating whose role it is to do what will save you a lot of pain in the Measure stage – particularly if certain things are not happening – because you can easily identify who is supposed to be doing it and rectify the situation.

The same applies to communicating what you are going to measure and how and for whom. Effective communication here will mean everyone knows what is being measured (which particular outcomes), how it is being measured (what method is being used to capture the data) and for whom (which stakeholder group are you measuring outcomes for).

This level of clarity needs to be communicated because the typical objections from people for not doing impact measurement are:

- I don't see why we have changed the survey/form.
- Why are we asking these questions?

By not only communicating what, how and for whom clearly but engaging with your stakeholders in making those decisions, they will be part of the process and it will make communication easier.

Communicating impact in the Measure Stage

When you are actually doing the data collection, the key thing to communicate here is:

- What are you doing with the data that's collected?

This question helps both the person who is collecting the data and also the person (or organisation or business) you are collecting data from. Thinking from the perspective of the person collecting the data – they know there's a reason why they are collecting the data (and this can be linked back to the questions in the define stage around why you are measuring impact and the benefits of doing this). So, being clear about what you'll do with the data gives the data collector confidence that they are not wasting their time (and that the data won't sit in a box or on a computer system never to be looked at). It also means they can explain clearly to the people they are collecting data from what will happen to the data, where it will be stored, how it will be anonymised, and how you'll respond to any responses that require action (such as negative feedback or outcomes).

Without going in to detail about GDPR and Data Protection you need to make sure you have consent to collect and process the data. If you capture case studies, videos, audio, photos or feedback quotes that you may want to publish then please make sure they have given permission for you to use them. If there is any doubt about consent (or a person's ability to give consent) then you need to exclude that person's data from your analysis.

Communicating impact in the Analyse Stage

Once you've captured the data you'll need to communicate what it is telling you. This is where communicating what success looks like in terms of impact will be important – because you can then compare your data to your idea of success. In the Analyse stage communication is focused on looking at the short-term and responding through making operational decisions quickly based on what the data is telling you regarding success. The key question here is:

- How will you know if you've been successful or not?

The easiest way to answer this question is to create some metrics for your organisation's impact. The crucial thing here is that they are your metrics – not ones that have been imposed by funders or commissioners. You must first decide what success looks like and then communicate that to your stakeholders – not the other way round.

This approach opens up dialogue and the likelihood that you don't end up reporting to lots of different funders and commissioners in different ways using different systems. You lead and direct the impact conversation based on your knowledge of how best to capture data to show if the activities are being delivered successfully.

The metrics can be percentages for positive outcomes (with a minimum level that needs to be achieved), maximum percentages for negative outcomes, levels of drop outs/numbers not completing the programme if appropriate, and any other issues/items that need investigating further. This data can then be communicated during team meetings with a view to identifying any issues and making changes quickly to your activities or the processes. It's best to make it a standing agenda item so impact is always on the agenda.

You can then communicate what you've achieved so far, what you're doing differently or what you've changed to the relevant stakeholders (customers, funders, commissioners etc.) so they can see that you're being pro-active in managing your impact on an on-going basis. This leads to regular reviews to see if your results are improving over time.

Communicating impact in the Learn Stage

The Learn stage focuses on the communication of your overall impact. It includes the learnings and connects these to your strategic development. The key questions in this stage are:

- How does it affect continual improvement and the organisation's future plans?
- How will you share the findings from the data?
- Who will you share the findings with?

This is where having a plan for how you'll share your impact findings with your stakeholders is crucial. The planning will identify if different stakeholders will want to know about different things and if you need to share the impact data differently depending on the stakeholder.

As sharing and communicating your impact is so important Chapters 18 and 19 are dedicated to the various methods you can use to effectively communicate impact internally and externally.

The other aspect of communication in this stage is internally around how impact affects your strategic direction and business planning. I talked about developing an Impact Led strategy in the previous Chapter, and this stage links to how this is communicated. By making impact the driver for conversations, it becomes a natural part of your communication.

To communicate what you have learnt impact needs to be discussed at your Board meetings. The focus here should be on what the data means in terms of new product or service development, gaps in delivery (that may require you to invest/spend more or that may require finding a partner to work with), and also how it impacts on your future strategy and financial position. In Chapter 18 I'll talk more about impact metrics for internal reporting to support you to embed impact.

CHAPTER 5: EMBEDDING IMPACT

The third cross cutting theme is embedding impact. Embedded is such an overused word these days, but its general meaning is 'fixed firmly and deeply to its surroundings' or 'implanted'. I like the idea of it being implanted because when impact is embedded, everyone in the organisation knows what impact you're trying to create, why you're measuring your impact, and is confident about how they contribute to creating impact. You also regularly discuss and report on your impact internally at team meetings and board meetings.

For most organisations having impact embedded to the extent that it is 'implanted' is very much an aspiration. In this Chapter you'll find out how you can move from an aspiration to really embedding impact in your organisation.

HOW TO EMBED IMPACT

Once you have identified your desired impact and the products or services that will allow you to achieve that (as discussed in Chapter 3), you then need to look at what needs to change within the business to make this happen.

Here are seven ways you start to embed impact right now:

Values
Your organisation's values are not only the shop window of your organisation, but the shelves, the stock, the till, the carrier bags, the absolute everything – that's why it's a great place to start.

Embedding impact into your values, therefore, needs to be embedded within the very people who are going to be representing them: your staff. Make sure your staff know what the organisation's values are, and are aligned to those values and share the same ethos as the leadership team.

Language
It is amazing how simple things like the language you use can really propel you into a certain way of thinking, which is why it is a crucial point for embedding impact.

Start to talk differently about what you do – talk in terms of impact, rather than activities and services. For example, instead of saying: "We provide healthcare" Try: "We help people to live as independently as possible." Or, to replace "We provide training", opt for "We enable people to achieve their career aspirations."

Training
Providing impact awareness training to your staff is the only way you are going to get them on board to join you in making as much impact as you desire (and to support your IMM activities) – after all – you can't do it alone.

Encouragement

After the training, encourage your staff to think independently about their own actions, and how they can add to, and enhance, the impact you achieve for your organisation and stakeholders. Listening to and actively encouraging your staff to contribute their opinions will give them a stronger sense of purpose and drive, which ultimately plays a huge part in successfully embedding impact.

Get the Board on board

Having the backing of your Board is not only great for ensuring everyone is working towards the same mission; it also means decision-making is more effective. By ensuring everyone is committed to including impact goals in meetings, you are more likely to embed it within the DNA of your organisation.

Measure

By having performance metrics to measure and keep track of your impact throughout the year, it will mean you can track your impact in the same way you do your financial performance.

Talk about it

Keep impact on the agenda of staff meetings, project reviews, appraisals and discussions. You can use the performance metrics mentioned above, as conversation starters. By doing this you will really embed it within your organisation's DNA.

THINKING ABOUT DEPARTMENTS

When you are embedding impact you will need to think about what the Operations, Facilities, Marketing, Sales, Finance & Management, HR and your organisation should look like if it is to solve the problem in the best way. If you do not have these separate departments, it is still worthwhile identifying how each area of your organisation needs to function.

Taking each department of your organisation in turn, ask yourself:

- What should this department look like?
- What would be required of it?
- How different is this to what you currently have in place?
- What facilities would you need to deliver your activities? Do you need to own property? Is an office, remote working or some other combination more effective?
- How will you transition to an impact led organisation?
- What financial and staff resources would be required to deliver this? Do you have these or do you need more/less?
- Would it be better to work with more/less people and have a greater impact?

For example, for Finance, it might mean looking at how resources are spent with impact being part of your decision-making criteria. For Facilities and Operations, it would include looking at how you need to deliver your activities to create the most impact. For Marketing and Sales – how can you encourage your customers (whether that is individuals, commissioners or funders) to take a long-term approach focused on achieving impact rather than outputs? This requires your marketing and sales pitch to explain why you are doing things differently.

The crucial area is Management and Organisation – this is where the values and ethos of the organisation are created. If management don't get what impact you are trying to create, and follow through by making decisions based on how you can maximise your impact, then that approach will filter down throughout the organisation, leading to a short-term output approach. To make this work, your management team and Board will have to have patience to explain it several times to people and organisations that may not understand the approach. The Board and Management team need to be comfortable with approaching business planning through an impact lens first, rather than the traditional approach. Finally, it is also your culture – the way the Board and Management team talk about your organisation is the way everyone else involved will talk about it. Are you talking impact and outcomes or outputs and activities?

In HR this would include shifting from having staff, volunteers and Board members who see their role as just providing an activity to seeing it as delivering impact. This means connecting what each person does to the impact the organisation has, so they can see the importance of their role and encouraging continuous improvement in order to achieve more impact. On a more basic level it would include having impact mentioned in job descriptions, setting objectives and goals for individuals that are linked to impact, and discussing these at appraisals as well as at regular reviews. As mentioned earlier, impact should also be a regular item for staff meetings as well as for Board meetings (see Chapter 8 on impact metrics for staff and Board meetings).

Chapter 6: Embedding Impact through Social Procurement

I have included a Chapter entirely on social procurement as this is a growing area of interest where organisations can increase the impact they have, and support other organisations or businesses to deliver greater impact through their supply chains.

The Background To Social Procurement

In the UK, The Public Services (Social Value Act) 2012[iii] moved social procurement up the agenda. There are similar things happening in other countries such as in Australia[iv], Canada[v], India, Spain, Germany and France where social procurement policies and frameworks are being implemented.

Within the UK, there are regional pieces of legislation that support the delivery of the Social Value Act in Wales and Scotland (The Well-being of Future Generations (Wales) Act 2015[vi] and the Community Benefits in Procurement for Scotland[vii]).

Social Value Act overview

The Public Services (Social Value Act) 2012 came in to being in January 2013, and it required public sector bodies to consider social value when procuring and commissioning services. Social value is essentially about how non-financial benefits can be achieved through commissioning and procurement that benefit people, the economy and the environment. The focus is on how every £1 that is spent can achieve more through the suppliers also delivering social value.

It marked massive progress in the way the public sector should think about who its suppliers are – and it was hoped it would open up the market to social enterprises and charities more because they were automatically delivering social value simply by existing because they are supporting people or the planet.

In reality, it didn't work that well – the majority of public sector commissioners didn't really understand it and most didn't implement it. Research in 2016 by SEUK showed only one in three councils considered social value and only 24% had a social value policy[viii]. There are some great examples of where it was implemented – such as Salford Council and Sandwell Council but most carried on as before. The reason for this was that it only required commissioners to consider social value – not actually include it.

There were also limits on when the Act applied. It didn't apply to contracts below the OJEU (The Official Journal European Union) threshold (currently this is c.£123,000 for central government contracts and c.£189,000 for other public sector bodies). This meant that many small, locally based social enterprises and charities would see no difference to the way services were commissioned for the size of contracts they would tender for. It also did not include works or goods.

Any social value criteria used needed to be relevant and proportionate to the value of the contract – meaning in most cases not much was required and inevitably large businesses could easily demonstrate they delivered as much (if not more) social value than social enterprises and charities could. The other issue was that very few commissioners actually followed up to see if the social value was delivered or if it was actually additional (i.e. for a lot of construction companies apprentices for young people were classed as added social value but in reality their business model is built around the use of apprentices anyway). Those that did implement it were often very focused on economic impact that could be delivered through contracts – typically focusing on job creation, apprenticeships and training, as well as spending locally, rather than the social impacts that social enterprises and charities are typically focused on delivering.

I know you are probably wondering why I'm sharing all this doom and gloom when I talked about how social procurement can increase impact at the start of the Chapter! Well – here is the good news. In the UK, in 2019, there was a consultation that aimed to make social value a requirement for any central government procurement. Despite Brexit and other things that happened during 2020, eventually in September 2020, the new measures were announced (and will take effect from January 2021)[ix].

If you are a supplier to central government or in a supply chain delivering a central government contract you will now need to evidence your social value. The bigger implication of these changes is that it will be introduced to local authorities and all public sector contracts eventually – increasing the importance of measuring impact and being able to prove the social value you create. 10% of the scoring for tenders (commissioners can allocate more if they wish) will be assigned to social value, and this means that any organisations in the supply chain will also have to evidence this – which will be a game changer – as it will filter down to every organisation and business eventually. By proactively focusing on creating impact and measuring it effectively you are in a much better position to evidence your social value than businesses that do not do this. Although these changes are not being introduced by amendments to the legislation they are now official guidance. If you are not based in the UK, the events of 2020 have seen a growing interest in developing procurement processes that are more sustainable, and that care about people and the planet – so I have no doubt that social procurement will grow globally over the coming years.

For the central government procurement the high-level themes and outcomes are:

The first theme is Covid-19 recovery – the focus here is employment, re-training and return to work; supporting people and communities to recover; supporting organisations and businesses to recover; health and reduced demand on public services (mainly in relation to mental health in the workplace); and workplace conditions.

The second theme is Tackling economic inequality – with the policy outcomes being focused on creating new businesses, new jobs and new skills (including entrepreneurship, growth and business creation, employment, education and training). The second outcome area is increasing supply chain resilience and capacity (through diverse supply chains, innovative and disruptive technologies, modernising delivery and increasing productivity, collaboration throughout the supply chain and managing cyber security risks).

Fighting climate change is the third theme, and the outcomes here are effective stewardship of the environment (delivering additional environmental benefits through the contract and influencing environmental protection and improvement).

Equal Opportunities is the fourth theme, and the outcome areas are reducing the disability employment gap (through increasing representation of disabled people in the workforce and supporting disabled people in developing new skills) and tackling workforce inequality (in the workforce, supporting in-work progression, and identifying and managing the risks of modern slavery).

The final theme is wellbeing. The outcome areas here are improving health and wellbeing (in the workforce and influencing support for health and wellbeing) and improving community integration (through collaboration in co-design and delivery, and influence to support strong, integrated communities).

Whilst these themes may look interesting – in reality most of the reporting metrics are focused on economic impacts. For the wellbeing theme, the outcome on improving community integration has a reporting metric of the number of people-hours spent supporting local community integration, such as volunteering and other community-led initiatives, under the contract. To me, that is not really going to evidence co-design or strong, integrated communities.

EMBEDDING IMPACT THROUGH YOUR OWN SOCIAL PROCUREMENT POLICY

For impact to be truly embedded in your organisation, it is about more than just measuring the impact your product, services or activities generate. It is also about being aware of the impact you have by simply existing as an organisation. This includes the impact you have on employees and volunteers, the impact you have through your purchasing decisions, your use of energy, your waste and recycling, the amount of travel you do etc.

That is why having a social procurement policy is vital. This provides you with a strategic approach to your purchasing and supply chain – that adds social value. By being strategic it will add impact in areas that align with your organisation's purpose and ultimate goal. There's nothing worse than tenders that ask suppliers to say what kind of social value they can deliver – the buyer should be specifying the type of social value they are interested in. If that has been your approach to date when putting out tenders – think about the types of social value your suppliers could deliver to your beneficiaries.

Now you understand why it matters, let's talk about how to go about it. First off, be clear about what your ultimate goal is – and then how this could be supported by your suppliers. By taking this approach it means through your supply chain you can increase the social value you deliver beyond what is created through your core activities. For example, if your ultimate goal is to eradicate food waste, then you could include donating food waste to local community organisations as one of the ways they can add social value to the contract. However, to date, most of the focus of social procurement policies tends to be on economic impact (through creating training, volunteering, work experience, apprenticeships and employment opportunities), as well as through buying locally.

An example of where procurement is aligned with purpose is a housing association that decided to encourage contractors that do repairs in their customers' homes to deliver social value by volunteering to teach the customers basic DIY and decorating skills. This helped the customers to maintain their homes and have a sense of belonging/ownership – which typically means there is less need for costly repairs by the housing association and the tenancy is sustained for longer. Another organisation asked its IT provider to offer recycled laptops to its beneficiaries to help them get online. Several organisations have asked for staff to volunteer as mentors to support their beneficiaries. There are lots of options if you think about what would add value to your existing delivery.

CREATING YOUR POLICY

With an idea of the types of social value you would like suppliers to deliver, you need to create your policy. This will include:

1. The key commitments you will deliver through your purchasing
2. How you will measure the success of your purchasing of social value
3. A simple framework that tells suppliers what you are looking for, tender limits, data collection requirements, and the monitoring you will undertake. This does not have to be complicated. If you are a small organisation, you can use a simple list of supplier must-haves/criteria to make purchasing decisions including:
   - Product is from sustainable sources
   - Clear anti modern day slavery details
   - Pays the Living Wage/is Living Wage Accredited
   - Able to volunteer time/contribute to your objectives
   - Zero waste policy in place

If you are larger and want to create a more complex procurement framework, then it is good to start with what you are expecting from suppliers. Many suppliers will not know much about social value, and those that do will not necessarily understand about additionality – and may decide to include social value that was going to be created anyway. That is why specifying the types of social value you want is better. You could also give suppliers the opportunity to suggest alternatives or innovative ways in which they believe they could deliver social value. A good example of a Social Value in Procurement Toolkit is from Bolton at Home[x].

Once you have developed your social procurement policy, please make sure you actually use it. It seems obvious – but unless everyone who makes purchases is aware of it – you may find some purchasers do not follow the policy. Second, monitor and check with your suppliers that the social value you agreed is being delivered, and if it isn't, then take action to get it delivered.

Social procurement is all about getting the most good out of your purchasing, therefore I believe it should always be a scored element of any tender response. Many tenders include social value as a non-scored part of the tender, and simply score quality and price. To have a workable social procurement policy, there should be different requirements depending on the size of the contract/tender. With bigger contracts requiring more social value, and for smaller purchases, where you are not using a formal tendering process, you can simply use your purchasing criteria.

SECTION 2: MEASURING IMPACT

CHAPTER 7: WHY BOTHER?

I am always asking, "Why don't more people bother to measure their impact?" In my experience, most people don't understand why they might want to measure their impact. It's always been presented as something that is forced upon organisations by funders or external agencies, and not usually something that an organisation opts to do.

Herein lies the biggest issue – it makes it appear as if impact measurement is something you have to do rather than something you would want to do. And, when you have to do something what usually happens? You come up with all sorts of excuses!

ALL THE EXCUSES

It's too complicated. Yes I agree there is a lot of information about that tries to make impact measurement seem really complex. If you choose to read about every available method (there are over 170 different methods) you would definitely end up confused. But the good news is you can use the five stage process in this book to remove the complexity.

It's too time consuming – it is if you think it's one person's job/role. Whereas if you build it into the existing systems, processes and everyone's jobs then it isn't. In Chapter 14 you will get to think about this more.

We don't have the resources – you don't need a full time monitoring and evaluation person – if you've had that perspective you're looking at it all wrong. Everyone is responsible for impact.

We don't have the expertise or don't know how to do it – you don't need a lot of expertise – you need to ask the right questions and capture the right data based on outcomes and impact, rather than outputs.

We have been around for decades and haven't had to measure the impact we deliver before. My response is "don't assume you are having an impact or making any positive change" – just because your business model is about doing something good it doesn't mean it's making a lasting difference to peoples' lives or the environment.

We aren't measured by outcomes or impact – so you're going to let external organisations decide what you do? Let's get real – don't you want to develop your products or services and continually improve what you do? Don't you want to be able to get money from customers more easily? Oh, ok, if the answer is no don't read any further!

And so on. You get the picture. But all these excuses seem crazy to me – it's a bit like trying to reduce your blood pressure but never measuring it – because you just think what you're doing is working. For me, I've found the biggest reason organisations don't do it is fear – fear that they will find out what they are doing is not that great or impactful. As with all messages about fear – you have got to feel the fear and do it anyway. It will be enlightening – as you'll be able to look at what's working and what's not and improve things (if you need to).

Let's bust a few myths about impact measurement and data while you are here:

- Your impact data does not need to be of a higher standard or quality than your other types of data
- You do not need to consult everyone
- You do not need to measure everything

If these myths were true then impact measurement would be a full time job, every organisation would be scared to publish their data for fear of external scrutiny and your data collection methods would be so complex they probably would not work in real life.

THE BENEFITS

Now let's think about the benefits of measuring and managing your impact:

- Better staff retention and engagement, and more understanding of your organisation's purpose
- Ability to market your organisation more easily – you have a compelling impact story
- Increasing levels of impact through continual improvement and delivery that is focused on impact not outputs
- Evidence for funding, contracts and investment – you can detail the impact you have

- Stakeholder engagement – it's a great way to have conversations with your various stakeholders and to get their input
- Strategic alignment – this is the biggie – your strategy becomes focused on delivering impact and the best ways you can do it, rather than simply delivering products or services.

WHY DO YOU WANT TO MEASURE YOUR IMPACT?

I talked about this in Chapter 4, but this crucial question is often overlooked, and it is important that you are clear about why you are measuring impact, and have identified the audience and the purpose for capturing impact data. Many organisations simply jump straight in and say we need to measure our impact, or we need some impact data for this project for a funder, and forget to step back and think strategically about impact measurement.

But, if you get clarity on why you want to do impact measurement, then it won't be a rushed or sped up thing, it will be part of your on-going processes and it will be planned. The end result will be that is adds more value to your organisation strategically too.

When I am working with organisations I ask them to prioritise the purpose of their impact measurement based on the following:

- To report back to a funder
- To communicate what you do and your impact
- To make sure you are operating effectively

- To identify where you can make improvements
- To evidence how you comply with the Social Value Act
- To identify the potential savings you make for the public sector
- To monetise your social value and calculate a SROI figure

Having a clear why will then assist with deciding what you want to focus on measuring:

- Your social impact
- Your environmental impact
- Your economic impact
- All three (social, economic and environmental impact)
- A specific project/area of your work

Then, finally, decide what your internal capacity to undertake impact measurement is, as this will give you an idea of how to structure the impact measurement.

- You have limited resources (time, money and staff) and are new to impact measurement
- You are experienced in using impact measurement systems
- You are committed to measuring your impact but staff have little time to implement this
- You have lots of data but currently don't do anything with it and need help to establish systems and ways to analyse this data

With clarity around these three areas you can start to dive in to measuring your impact. These questions are included in the free downloadable resources – in the Social Value Checklist (see the Free Resources section at the end of the book). Of course, for some of you, the purpose and areas of focus will be funder led, but this really does miss the opportunity to achieve so much more. The following Chapters focus on the five stages of the Lean Social Impact Approach.

CHAPTER 8: DEFINE

Define is the first stage of the Lean Social Impact Approach. In this stage you define your ultimate goal. You may refer to this as your vision or mission, and is the big picture view of what the world looks like if you are successful. It should not describe the activities, products or services you deliver. It should be focused on the difference those activities, products or services make. If you have started on developing an Impact Led Strategy (see Chapter 3) you will hopefully have defined your ultimate goal.

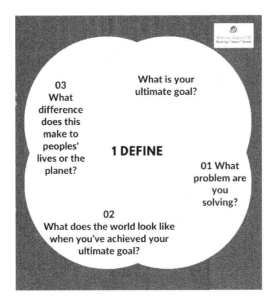

This is by far the most important part of the Lean Social Impact Approach, as it sets you up nicely to put all your ducks in a row to simplify your impact measurement. It sounds easy but very often organisations are created to deliver a product or service, and the longer-term purpose has not been thought about.

To start the process of defining your ultimate goal, answer these three questions:

1. What problem are you solving?
2. What does the world look like when you have achieved your ultimate goal?
3. What difference does this make to peoples' live and/or the planet?

Once you've answered these questions, look for common themes and then write out your ultimate goal as a statement - ideally around 15 words. Examples include:

- A world where all businesses are social enterprises that positively impact people and the planet (that's our vision at Make an Impact CIC)
- A world without poverty
- Equal rights for everyone
- People live happy and fulfilled lives
- Achieving a sustainable world for all
- Developing a circular economy
- Enabling people to achieve their full potential

(As you'll notice these are what I call "big picture" goals, and that's what you need to identify for your organisation).

Things that aren't great ultimate goals are:

- Providing employment for people
- Improving wellbeing

The reason these aren't great ultimate goals is because they're unlikely to be the ultimate goal – for example, in most cases employment achieves some other ultimate goal for the individual (such as increased income, better opportunities for the future). The same applies to wellbeing outcomes, or engaging people in sports or outdoor activities.

Not sure you have identified your ultimate goal? Ask yourself this question, "So what, what difference does that make?" When you can't come up with another answer you've found your ultimate goal.

Can you have more than one ultimate goal? Occasionally, your organisation may have two diverse purposes so developing one ultimate goal can be difficult. In this situation you would have two ultimate goals. I generally do not recommend more than two ultimate goals, as this can create a lack of focus around the types of impact you deliver, and subsequently a lack of focus when looking at your organisational development.

SUSTAINABLE DEVELOPMENT GOALS

You can use the Sustainable Development Goals to help you identify your ultimate goal. The Sustainable Development Goals (SDGs) are 17 Global Goals that countries are working towards achieving by 2030. Across these 17 goals there are 169 targets and 230 indicators.

Although the SDGs do not cover every possible impact, if you think one of the goals might be relevant then visit the SDG website[xi] and see if there are specific targets that are relevant under that goal. Using the SDGs in this way will give a focus to your impact measurement. For example, if Goal 1: No Poverty looked relevant for your organisation, you would then need to see which specific targets you are working towards, such as:

Target 1.1 – By 2030, eradicate extreme poverty for all people everywhere, currently measured as people living on less than $1.25 a day. By choosing this specific target it means you can track and measure how many people move out of extreme poverty as a consequence of your activities. This is far better than simply saying your organisation is reducing poverty, but you have no metrics or data to prove by how much.

I often see UK based organisations using the SDGs to report their impact against – by claiming they've supported 300 people out of poverty, but it is unlikely that the work in the UK has targeted the people the SDGs were designed to improve life for. They are intended to bring the world's poorest people out of poverty (which is only a very small proportion of the UK's population) and so the organisation has not really delivered anything against the no poverty SDG. This links very nicely to the principle of not over-claiming – and so far what I've seen around SDG reporting is over-claiming by UK based organisations. Many use Buy One Give One models where they give a micro loan, water or training course to someone in a poorer country, and these are counted against the different SDGs. Again, I'm not sure of the validity of this – does giving someone water for a day count as achieving something against the SDGs – or are we talking about long-term sustainable changes? I like to believe we are talking long-term sustainable change because it's in the name (SDG) and if that's the case we should only be counting things against SDGs that are sustained.

The SDGs can help your organisation (even if it's really small) connect to the bigger picture and get clarity about the big goal(s) you are working towards. The goals also provide a framework for you if you are struggling to move from what you do on a day-to-day basis to seeing what the wider impact is. For some of you, you will decide the goals seem too big and make what you're doing seem insignificant. I'd encourage you to move away from this thinking – as each small sustainable contribution creates huge change.

However, before you get too excited about the SDGs there are a couple of flaws with them. Whilst the SDGs can potentially provide you with your ultimate goal and outcomes for a theory of change (see Chapter 9 for more details about theory of change), they do not replace the need to have a proper system for measuring your impact.

Secondly, the SDGs address global problems and issues, and whilst they are globally important, and each country has its own priorities, there may be regional, or local problems that are more important to address that are not direct targets within the 17 goals. So, if you do decide to use the SDGs for your ultimate goal or the outcomes you measure, please bear in mind how best to use the SDGs so you are truly delivering against them.

NEXT STEPS

Once you have answered the three questions in the Define stage and created a short statement to summarise your ultimate goal, it is very beneficial to share and discuss this with your key stakeholders, and obtain feedback. Then you can move on to work on developing your theory of change.

CHAPTER 9: THEORY OF CHANGE

A theory of change is a simplified process for an activity, product or service or for your whole organisation showing the outcomes and impact that you are planning to deliver. It is an idea of how you think change will happen – and is a bit like a route map showing how you will get to your ultimate goal. A theory of change is useful once you are clear about why you are measuring your impact and have defined your ultimate goal.

The key things about a theory of change are:

It is a theory so it does not mean that things will necessarily happen exactly as you anticipate. Some of the complexity of real life and how change happens are lost through simplifying it. A theory of change generalises the process (so try not to think of specific individuals, as you will end up creating a different theory of change for each person).

It is focused on change and putting it in to a linear process. You and I both know that change is not always linear, and people have different starting points and different end points. Nevertheless, theories of change are the generally accepted model and approach to mapping out what change you expect to see happen across the sector, so you do really need to create one.

MAPPING YOUR THEORY OF CHANGE

You may have more than one theory of change – for example, an organisational one that focuses on the core outcomes and ultimate goal of your organisation, and more detailed theories of change for each of your programmes/activities.

For me, a theory of change, forms part of the development of an impact led strategy – because its focus is on your ultimate goal and then finding solutions (through products, services, activities and projects) to successfully achieve that goal. By working backwards, a theory of change highlights the activities you need to deliver to achieve your outcomes and you can see the way outcomes connect to each other too. For example, an outcome of an individual gaining employment may have intermediary outcomes including improved confidence and motivation that have to happen before the individual gains employment. If you have a number of activities focused on improving confidence but nothing around motivation the theory of change can help you to decide if you need to redesign your activities.

To develop your theory of change ask the different stakeholders what changes are important to them and what difference your organisation has made to them. This is called mapping the theory of change. Unlike a typical business planning process that starts with your products or services, mapping a theory of change works backwards from the ultimate goal. Then you identify all the intermediary changes (outcomes) and then the activities/services/products.

Usually, the senior management team, Board, staff and other key stakeholders create the theory of change. Ideally, you need to include a range of stakeholders and people that are actually involved in delivery – so the theory can be as accurate as possible. Most people map their theory of change by getting their key stakeholders together and holding a short workshop where they go through this process with them. You can map your theory of change using post-it notes and paper, or you can use online tools and develop it collaboratively. Better Evaluation has an article[xii] that shares details of some online tools. I have included a free Theory of Change Worksheet for you to download (see Free Resources section), and use Miro to create theories of change online.

Many organisations will have produced stakeholder maps, which detail 30-40 stakeholders, but let's continue to keep it simple, and group your stakeholders as follows:

- Clients/Customers/Beneficiaries/service users (these could be broken down in to sub-groups such as workshop attendees, young people etc.)
- Volunteers
- Staff
- Board members
- Partner organisations
- Funder/Commissioners
- Local community

From this list, think about the top three stakeholder groups that you want to include in the theory of change. This means including the changes that happen for these three stakeholder groups in your theory of change. For example if you selected your beneficiaries, staff and a funder as your three stakeholder groups, they may each have different priorities for a wellbeing programme. The beneficiaries may be interested in socialising more and feeling less isolated, the staff may be interested in helping the beneficiaries to self manage their mental health and wellbeing, and the funder may be interested in community connectivity. These differing changes would be reflected in the theory of change, and contribute to the ultimate goal of people leading more fulfilled lives.

Working with three stakeholder groups means the mapping process does not become overwhelming (and that's before you have started trying to capture data from your different stakeholder groups). There is no point trying to consult everyone if you have not done any consultation previously, so focus on the key stakeholders first. You can consult other stakeholder groups in future cycles of your impact measurement process. Once you have chosen your key stakeholder groups, start mapping your theory of change. Typically, there will be many changes and it is important to work out what order these changes happen in, as well as what activities led to which changes using the process on the following page.

When trying to identify the outcomes that occur for your key stakeholders there are two main types – hard and soft outcomes. Hard outcomes are those that are easy to define and measure (and are easily quantifiable) such as getting a job, completing a training course and getting a house. Hard outcomes are either achieved or not, and there is no middle ground. Soft outcomes are less tangible and are usually more difficult to measure. They involve the individual's (or your) perception of what has changed, such as self-esteem, resilience and motivation. Soft outcomes typically focus on progression. In many cases, the soft outcomes highlight the real impact you have by providing the detail behind the hard outcomes – so one without the other does not tell your full impact story.

THE THEORY OF CHANGE PROCESS

What is the ultimate goal you achieve?

What are the intermediary changes that have to happen to reach your ultimate goal?

What activities are delivered to achieve these changes?

Which activity leads on to which change? And which change leads on to another change?

Which changes lead to the ultimate goal?

Check your assumptions and the process

EXAMPLE THEORY OF CHANGE

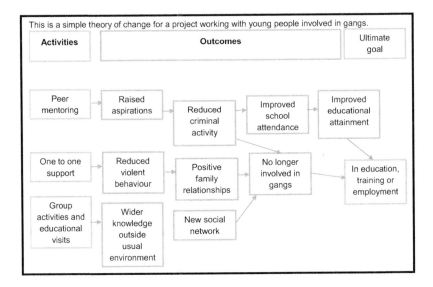

This is a simple theory of change for a project working with young people involved in gangs.

Activities	Outcomes	Ultimate goal

Peer mentoring → Raised aspirations → Reduced criminal activity → Improved school attendance → Improved educational attainment

One to one support → Reduced violent behaviour → Positive family relationships → No longer involved in gangs → In education, training or employment

Group activities and educational visits → Wider knowledge outside usual environment → New social network

NEXT STEPS

Once you have created your theory of change you can move on to the second stage of the Lean Social Impact Approach – which is focused on planning what outcomes you will measure. After this, you will identify what data needs to be collected to evidence that the outcomes have happened. Through the data collection you can see if you are achieving the outcomes you expected, as well as any unexpected outcomes (both positive and negative), and if not, ask questions to find out why and to improve your outcomes as part of a cycle of continuous improvement. The theory of change is not static – as you gather data, you should update it to reflect what is actually happening.

CHAPTER 10: PLAN

S
o far, you have worked through the Define stage and identified your ultimate goal as well as mapping your theory of change. The second stage of the Lean Social Impact Approach - the Plan stage - is the stage where a lot of the hard work happens. It is also the stage with the most content in this book – as it is covering how you will actually do the measuring to prove you are achieving your ultimate goal.

The best advice I can give you is to say "plan" – plan your data collection processes and then implement them. All too often there is no planned process and it means that valuable impact data is often lost along the way. It also means you don't know what potential issues there are with your activities either.

To complete this stage the three questions are:

1. What two key changes (outcomes) have to happen to achieve your ultimate goal?
2. How will you know these outcomes have been achieved?
3. What data do you need to collect, how often and how will you collect it?

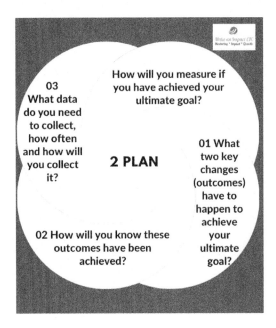

You have probably got lots of stakeholders, but let's get real here, you have avoided doing impact measurement up until now - or not really focussed on it properly – so planning to consult and collect data from lots of stakeholder groups is very unlikely to happen. By choosing just two stakeholder groups to capture impact data from it means you can actually get started without being overwhelmed.

Once you have identified who the two are, it's time to identify the outcomes that matter most to these two stakeholder groups. If you did not include the stakeholders in your theory of change mapping process you will need to find out what the priority outcomes are now. These outcomes can be identified by talking to the stakeholder groups, or to staff members who are involved in delivery of activities that have an understanding of the stakeholder groups. You could also run a focus group or short consultation activity to bring together your key stakeholders to think about what outcomes matter to them. Providing you don't let one person speak or lead the conversation, and everyone gets the opportunity to share the outcomes that are important to them you will get an accurate reflection of the outcomes you need to measure.

Once you have gathered this information, the next step is then to prioritise the list of outcomes your stakeholders have told you about. Again, it's easiest to get your stakeholders to do this, rather than you assuming which should be ranked higher. A quick and easy way to do this if the people are physically present is to have the outcomes listed on a sheet, and give each person two stickers and ask them to put them next to the two outcomes they consider to be the most important. You can also do this via emails or surveys – where you send the list of outcomes and ask them to rank them in priority order. You can then collate the responses.

This will give you the basis for what you'll measure. If you have lots of outcomes, then I'd suggest measuring two per stakeholder group to start with (or an absolute maximum of three if you're struggling to narrow it down to two). You may be scared of measuring the wrong things, but it is better to measure something, realise what you are doing isn't quite right and change it, rather than doing nothing. It's also vitally important not to take the opposite approach and try to measure everything! Focus is crucial – and that's where knowing what the most important outcomes are to your key stakeholders is useful. I encourage you to imagine you are in a lift with one of your stakeholders, and you only have until they get out of the lift to ask them some questions about impact. What would you prioritise and focus on?

For the other outcomes that you do not choose to measure you can share these through case studies, feedback and qualitative data. You are probably already capturing data on your key stakeholder groups' characteristics, but if you are not, then think about what is relevant (such as a person's age, location, gender, health conditions or other characteristics) so you can segment them further and see if this affects the outcomes that are achieved. Stakeholder groups are not homogeneous and treating them as such can miss the differences in outcomes for many of that group. This is important for equality and diversity data, so you can see if your products or services are not as effective for certain parts of the community – and then you can make appropriate changes (see Chapter 15 for more details on this).

In future data collection cycles you may want to consider asking other stakeholders, or including those you may not know about. You can do this by asking existing stakeholder groups if there is anyone else you should consult or anyone else that has been impacted as a result of them being supported/your organisation's work. If they identify other stakeholder groups you were unaware of you can then talk to them about the impact you have on them. But for now let's focus on two outcomes for two stakeholder groups (that's four things to measure).

An alternative way to identify the priority outcomes is to look at your theory of change, and focus on the outcomes closest to the ultimate goal. The reason for this is that the earlier outcomes lead on to these later outcomes, so if you achieve the outcomes closest to the ultimate goal it is likely those earlier stage outcomes have been achieved too. For example, if you're helping people to self-manage their health conditions, then measuring how confident they feel in managing their health condition might be useful, whereas measuring changes in the access to support networks might not.

NEXT STEPS

Now you have answered the first question of the Plan stage (What two key changes (outcomes) have to happen to achieve your ultimate goal?) the following Chapters focus on the second and third questions in the Plan stage. These are How will you know these outcomes have been achieved? and What data do you need to collect, how often and how will you collect it?

CHAPTER 11: SOCIAL IMPACT AND COMMUNITY IMPACT

C hapter 11 is where you start to get in to the detail around your outcomes. Now you have identified the outcomes you want to measure, you need to figure out how you will know the outcomes have been achieved. These are often called 'indicators' or, as I prefer, the 'way of knowing' that an outcome has been achieved. In this Chapter, I will be sharing some resources, example questionnaires and surveys to help you identify the indicators for particular outcomes, and a range of ways you can measure social and community impacts.

STARTING PLACE

For starters, I recommend you look at the Big Society Capital's Outcome Matrix[xiii] or National TOMs[xiv] for identifying outcomes and indicators. Big Society Capital's Outcomes Matrix has an extensive list of outcomes and indicators that splits between social and community impacts and is useful if you are struggling to think of the indicator. Big Society Capital's Outcome Matrix is not great for all soft outcomes, as the indicators for these are not as well defined in their matrix. For soft outcomes, you may need to be more creative, but hopefully this Chapter will give you lots of ideas about what you can measure and how you can measure it.

The National TOMS has five core themes (jobs: local skills and employment, growth of responsible business, healthier, safer and more resilient communities, environmental impact and sustainable procurement, and promoting innovation).

Indicators can be a variety of things – so you do need to pick an indicator that is appropriate for the outcome you are trying to measure. You also need to make sure the indicator is suitable for your organisation and is something that you can measure relatively easily without it taking too much time or being too difficult to capture the data – otherwise you will have no impact data, or such a small amount you will not have a sufficient sample size.

TYPES OF SOCIAL IMPACT

Social impact is all about the changes you make to peoples' lives, so a lot of the changes are difficult to measure because they are soft outcomes (changes in a person's behaviour, attitudes or beliefs). For example, if you're delivering training or providing people with new skills/knowledge it is useful to measure if they know about or have learnt a particular skill. But the most important thing is whether they actually do anything with that new knowledge or skill – so you need to measure if their behaviour, attitudes or beliefs have changed to verify that the outcome is likely to be sustained beyond the few hours they are involved in the training.

To confirm changes in behaviours, attitudes or beliefs you will need to get the person to self-rate or score themselves or you will need to record the changes you are seeing in the person. I have included a few examples of social outcomes and possible indicators. As you will see, some of these are easier to identify as having happened, whereas others are harder to measure:

Outcome	Indicator
Improved budgeting	Able to pay bills on time, able to save some money each month
Improved confidence	Self-rated score, staff recorded, changes in outcomes star scores
Job readiness	Has a CV, has completed interview techniques training
Improved physical or mental health	Exercises more frequently, weight loss, self-rated feeling more positive about the future
Increased social networks, connections or peer support	Socialises more frequently, has someone to turn to in a crisis
Reduced re-offending	Levels of criminal activity

Reduced drug/alcohol misuse	Levels of drug/alcohol use, completion of detox programme
In to permanent housing	Has a secure home

Measuring Wellbeing

One of the areas that is popular for organisations to want to measure is wellbeing. You need to be clear about what you mean by wellbeing. This is because wellbeing is often seen as a homogeneous outcome when in reality wellbeing is not one outcome. Wellbeing is made up of a number of components and rather than saying you improve wellbeing you need to understand what specific aspects of wellbeing have improved. There are a many models that explain what wellbeing is. These are helpful for you to identify which areas of wellbeing you specialise in. The New Economics Foundation's National Accounts of Wellbeing[xv] include the wellbeing questions used in the European Social Survey, and covers:

- Supportive relationships
- Resilience and self-esteem
- Emotional wellbeing (positive feelings and absence of negative feelings)
- Life satisfaction
- Vitality
- Positive functioning (autonomy, meaning and purpose, engagement and competence)
- Trust and belonging
- Wellbeing at work

By identifying which of these areas of wellbeing you are delivering you can be more specific about which outcomes you measure. The Centre for Wellbeing at nef created a handbook[xvi] that is a guide to measuring wellbeing, which includes three recommended sets of questions for measuring wellbeing. The first being the SWEMWBS[xvii] (Short Warwick-Edinburgh Mental Well-being Scale) which is a set of seven questions that many organisations use for measuring wellbeing. The second is the Office for National Statistics (ONS) subjective wellbeing questions (a set of four questions on happiness, anxiety, satisfaction with life and the extent to which you feel the things you do in your life are worthwhile, that are included in the Household Survey in the UK) and the third a social trust question. If you use the ONS questions you will also be able to benchmark you wellbeing levels against those for your local authority and country. If you use all three sets of recommended questions there are 12 questions in total – which you may decide is too many to ask – and if that is the case then focus on the priority aspects of wellbeing for your stakeholders. Another good resource for measuring wellbeing is the Happiness Pulse website[xviii].

Workplace Wellbeing

The other aspect of wellbeing is your staff and volunteers' wellbeing (or workplace wellbeing). For many of you, you may provide apprenticeships, volunteering opportunities, work placements, training and employment for your beneficiaries, and being able to track their wellbeing in the workplace will help you to identify if you are providing the right support in their roles. The same applies for any non-beneficiary staff and volunteers. Workplace wellbeing includes things like:

- Flexible or remote working options
- Appropriate working conditions and equipment
- Expectations and work volumes
- Stress levels
- How you treat your staff
- Managerial support etc.

What Works Wellbeing have identified five main drivers[xix] of wellbeing in the workplace. These are in order of importance: health and relationships (both drivers ranked of equal importance), followed by security and environment (both drivers ranked of equal importance), then purpose. Their site includes a question bank for measuring workplace wellbeing, as well as a step-by-step guide and survey builder.

Health and social care

Health and social care is an area I have done a lot of impact measurement in, and includes changes in usage of drugs, alcohol, smoking, exercising, dietary changes, as well as management and awareness of health conditions, support for carers and respite, services for people with learning difficulties and disabilities, and much more. If you are delivering on behalf of the health service or mental health services, then the outcomes are often focused on reducing usage of acute services (such as emergency services within hospitals and GPs), and equipping individuals with the skills to self-manage their health conditions at home, and to become more independent.

Many established tools exist for measuring health and social care outcomes. You should refer to these when choosing questions for your own impact measurement. These include the PAM[xx] (Patient Activation Measure) to identify if patients have the knowledge, skills and confidence to manage their health condition. The Adult Social Care Outcomes Tool to measure quality of life in relation to social care (including personal cleanliness, comfort and dignity, control over daily life, accommodation cleanliness, personal safety, food and drink, as well as other outcomes).[xxi] For anxiety and depression, SDQs (Strengths and Difficulties Questionnaires)[xxii] can be used adults and children/their parents for very young children. There are also RCADS (Revised Children's Anxiety and Depression Scale)[xxiii] that are completed young people from the age of eight and their parents. The SCORE-15[xxiv] is a good questionnaire for looking at family functioning. The Treatment Outcomes Profile (TOP)[xxv] is for measuring outcomes for substance misuse services. As well as these specific questionnaires, there are a number of other resources including The Social Workers Toolbox[xxvi] which has many useful surveys around autism, drugs, parenting, self-harm and more. CAFCASS[xxvii] also has lots of questionnaires for working with children and adults around feelings and relationships. For young carers the Carers Trust has created a manual with questions and outcomes[xxviii] and for adult carers PSSRU created a set of questions to look at carer's experiences.[xxix]

Employment and barriers to employment

With soft outcomes, you may also hear the phrase distance travelled used, to represent the progress that is made in developing a new behaviour, attitude, belief or skill, and is commonly used when talking about job readiness. If you are interested in measuring job/work related skills and barriers to employment such as childcare, time keeping, interview skills, CV production, motivation to work etc. then the Journey to Employment (JET) Framework[xxx] is a good resource. Although it is designed for use with young people, many of the questions are relevant for all age groups. Many organisations that provide job readiness or access to employment, tend to focus on measuring the number of individuals who gain accredited qualifications or get jobs. This is often because that is what you are being paid to deliver, but I recommend you also track some key employability or job readiness soft outcomes as well. To do this think about the beneficiary's journey to achieving a qualification or employment – what skills do they develop along the way that you want to measure? Also, be clear about what you consider to be sustainable employment – is it a job that lasts six months, one year or longer?

Volunteering

Generally, you will have two types of volunteers – those that want to volunteer long-term and those that see volunteering as a stepping-stone to something else (and will probably volunteer for a shorter period). The long-term volunteers will have different motivations and outcomes from volunteering to those that are looking to move on. This makes it useful to identify why people want to volunteer. The JET Framework (mentioned above) has some useful questions around volunteering, including peoples' motivations for wanting to volunteer (such as to develop a new skill and to meet new people) and questions to identify what outcomes they have achieved through volunteering. These questions help you to understand what impact volunteering has for the volunteers. In terms of the impact of volunteers on your organisation, if you record the total hours of volunteering you can multiply this by the living wage to give you a monetary value that your volunteers contribute. There is also a wellbeing component to volunteering, and What Works Wellbeing has developed a theory of change[xxxi] around this – although it is difficult to prove that volunteering directly leads to improved wellbeing – it is clear that a sense of connectedness and a sense of purpose that volunteering may provide an individual do contribute to improved wellbeing.

Confidence

Another area of social impact is changes in confidence. With confidence, rather than asking if confidence has improved, is it better if you ask about confidence in a specific area (such as confidence in speaking to new people, confidence in managing their health condition, confidence in cooking, confidence in playing a musical instrument etc.).

Relationships

You may wish to measure changes in relationships with others. For example, having healthy boundaries in relationships which includes being able to say no, speaking up, not going along with what others say or want to do when you do not want to, and understanding what healthy relationships look like. Positive family relationships – this typically focuses on spending quality time together doing (fun) things, helping one another and being able to talk to each other about problems. The most common area of relationships is linked to wellbeing and focuses on having a support network. This covers having someone to turn to in a crisis, socialising with others outside of work/family, participating in hobbies/local groups, and knowing where to go for help. If you are focused on child-parent violence, there are useful questions to track changes in these relationships in the RCPV Evaluation Framework Child to Parent Violence[xxxii].

Offender management

With offender management you can measure changes in the specific crime (repeat offending rates) as well as looking at the offender pathways that measure areas that help to prevent re-offending (Accommodation, Education, training and employment, Health, Drugs and alcohol, Finance, benefit and debt, Children and families and Attitudes, thinking and behaviour). Clinks provides a guide that links to other toolkits you can use to measure change[xxxiii] as well as other useful resources for organisations working in the criminal justice system.

Beneficiary specific

If you are looking for outcomes for specific groups of beneficiaries (such as carers, young people, those with Autism or ADHD, new mums, victims of crime etc.) then I suggest looking at the Outcomes Stars[xxxiv]. There are about 40 different Stars that have been designed and tested with each beneficiary group. You do need to complete Star training and hold licences for staff to use the Star.

TYPES OF COMMUNITY IMPACT

Community impact includes outcomes that affect more than one individual or family, and reflect changes to a whole community, neighbourhood or area, or how individuals perceive that area.

Community cohesion

As with wellbeing, it is important to understand how you and your stakeholders define community cohesion, and what the most important elements are. The following are potential elements of community cohesion (which built upon the definition of community cohesion from the Cantle Report[xxxv] in 2001):

- Interdependence
- Shared loyalty
- Social ties/community commitments that bind people together
- Common vision/sense of belonging
- Appreciation of diversity and different backgrounds
- Similar life opportunities for all people not dependent on background
- A community where strong relationships can develop between people of different backgrounds at school and at work, as well as in the broader community

Whilst this list is great at stating what community cohesion is, when it comes to measuring it, you will need indicators to prove that there has been a change in community cohesion. For example, with a sense of belonging you could measure the levels of interaction between neighbours, how often people offer support or help to others, and the level of acceptance of diversity within the community, as well as whether there is a sense of pride and belonging in the local area.

Community engagement and access to resources

Community engagement which can be measured by the level of volunteering (although do be careful with this as demographics play a part in the likelihood that people will volunteer which can give a misleading figure for community engagement), as well as the use of local services and engagement in community events. In terms of access to resources, this is about the local built environment being accessible, as well as having access to open spaces, arts and cultural activities, sports facilities, public transport, and adequate and appropriate services. These are potentially easier to measure (as you can identify if the facilities etc. are available locally) but in terms of accessibility that would require you to ask local people.

Safety

Feeling safe, or having a perception of safety, can be measured in two ways. First, by looking at crime rates in the local area, and second, by asking local people how safe they feel their community is. This is best carried out a street by street level (either physically or using a map in a group setting), so you can identify any areas which are not considered safe by local people, and the track to see if your activities make any difference to how safe people feel.

Arts, heritage and culture

These areas are activities are very wide and diverse, and it would be impossible to cover every possibility here. The Arts Council[xxxvi] has useful guidance on potential outcomes, starting with a framework that looks at the following generic outcomes, which are then further broken down:

- Skills
- Knowledge and Understanding
- Behaviour and Progression
- Enjoyment, Inspiration and Creativity
- Attitudes and Values

The Heritage Lottery Fund[xxxvii] focuses on the accessibility of heritage, as well as how this leads to people having new skills, changes in ideas and actions, improved wellbeing and more people being engaged in local heritage. For youth music based projects, there is a guide to outcomes by Youth Music[xxxviii]. This includes instrumental skills, musical expression, performance skills, lyric writing skills and more. There is an interesting short report on the social outcomes from cultural activities, which includes 50 possible outcomes from cultural and arts activities[xxxix], which are wide ranging from providing a source of enjoyment to creating community traditions in new neighbourhoods, through to involving local people in the regeneration process. On the National Lottery Community Fund website, a link to further resources includes has a downloadable framework[xl]. This details how a wide range of outcomes can be measured.

For arts, heritage and cultural activities, the important thing is to recognise the distinction between one off, medium and long-term activities. For example, for events or exhibitions, the outcomes may be linked to raising awareness of particular issues, bringing people together and sharing of experiences. Whereas, medium or long-term activities may lead to increases in how people use their creativity in their everyday lives, a sense of belonging and community connectivity. Many organisations I have worked with use arts activities to bring different groups together to create shared understanding and history, develop new perspectives and views of one another, and improve wellbeing (such as inter-generational projects, and people from different ethnicities and cultural backgrounds).

PRODUCTS WITH SOCIAL OR COMMUNITY IMPACT

For product based organisations, it is often difficult to say that your product had a specific impact on peoples' lives – such as improving their health – because there will have been many contributing factors not just the fact that they now, for example, drink a healthier drink each day. The Customer experience questions (developed by the Impact Management Project)[xli] are useful to help you identify if your product does have any impact, as well as what impact customers were potentially hoping to achieve through their purchase.

USING THE SDGS

You can track and measure your progress against the SDGs (please refer back to Chapter 8 for more information on the SDGs). You can look at country specific data[xlii] and progress against the SDGs, as well as tracking your organisation's action and progress against a particular goal[xliii]. The SDG Impact Assessment Tool[xliv] is a self assessment process to identify your contribution to the SDGs. Finally, the SDG Compass[xlv] lists a range of tools that can be used for specific goals.

GENERAL QUESTIONS

If you are unsure about the social or community impact you create, you may want to ask general or open ended questions. Here are a few examples that you can make specific to the types of activities you deliver. Or alternatively, simply have conversations with your beneficiaries, as this will provide you with lots of valuable information.

- What has changed in your life since you started attending our project?
- How much of the change would you say is due to the support/services we have provided?
- How much have the following changed in your life...?

- Other than what you have mentioned already, have there been any other changes (positive or negative) in your life?
- Has anyone else (in your family) been affected by the changes you have experienced?
- How confident do you feel about...?
- Do you know how to do.../How often do you do the following...?

If you decide to do this, it's best to follow a two stage process – ask open ended questions to gather a wide range of outcome information from your stakeholders first. Then in subsequent questionnaires, you can incorporate checklists, specific questions or statements as you will have identified the outcomes. Always keep an "other" box just in case there is an outcome you have missed.

NEXT STEPS

Look at the relevant resources for the outcomes you are interested in measuring. Chapter 12 covers economic, environmental and tech impacts. Once you know how you will prove a particular outcome has been achieved, you can think about how to collect the data in Chapter 13.

CHAPTER 12: ECONOMIC, ENVIRONMENTAL AND TECH IMPACT

This Chapter covers economic, environmental and tech impact, which are generally easier to measure than social and community impacts. These impacts can relate to the core activities you deliver or can be a result of the fact that your organisation exists (for example, economic or environmental impacts you deliver through your social procurement policy or by employing people). I have included tech (technology) impact as due to many activities moving online this is an area of impact that is receiving more interest.

ECONOMIC IMPACT

Economic impact is about the economy and the financial circumstances of the people you work with, as well as the economic impact your organisation creates by existing in the world. Whilst social impact tends to be the area most organisations focus on, the economic impact is the one that public sector bodies and governmental agencies are often most interested in achieving. By existing as an organisation you have an economic impact whether you intended to or not. This includes things like:

- Employing people
- Paying suppliers/making purchases
- Owning or renting property
- Using premises/venues
- Bringing money in to communities/areas
- Winning contracts/funding
- Taking out loans or investment
- Paying the Living Wage (or not)
- Providing work experience, training and qualifications

The above are economic impacts you will have by existing, but depending on what your day-to-day activities are, you may also have a core economic impact that enables individuals to improve their economic situation, such as:

- Business start-up and growth support
- Apprenticeships
- Employment support services/access to employment
- Training and qualifications
- Money or debt advice

Economic impact is one of the easier areas to measure because many of the changes are considered hard outcomes (in that they are easy to identify as having happened). Things like getting a job, spending more money locally or reducing an individual's debt levels are things that are easy to know have happened.

To track the progress you will need to capture the right information at the start, by capturing some basic information about the individual or your organisation, including:

- Employment status
- Highest qualification levels
- Debt levels
- Money spent with local suppliers/social enterprises

Then following your support you would re-measure these items to check for changes. You can also track the following to calculate economic impact:

- Hours volunteered
- New contracts/funding/investment secured
- Additional jobs created
- Training provided

The National TOMS[xiv] is a helpful tool for measuring economic impact, including that of your supply chain.

If you are working with businesses or organisations, to either support them to start-up or grow, you could measure changes in the following:

- Income/turnover levels
- Profitability
- Number of new products/services to market
- Number of new jobs created
- Job retention levels and staff turnover
- Investment secured
- Contracts won

ENVIRONMENTAL IMPACT

Again, similar to economic impact, environmental impact can be a direct result of your core activities, or a consequence of how you run your organisation. For those of you trying to achieve environmental impact through your activities, pro-environmental behaviour scales[xlvi] are useful to see how much consumers are changing their behaviour towards the environment. These can be used for all types of activities including to see if anyone tries new environmentally conscious things after reading your blog; through to recycling levels, growing their own food, buying seasonal food, buying recycled items etc. There are lots of carbon calculators you can use with beneficiaries such as CoGo's real time carbon footprint tracker[xlvii] and thredUP's Fashion Footprint calculator[xlviii]. You can also look at system change around environmental policies, supply chains, modern day slavery and waste/carbon consumption. To do this it is important to recognise that you are potentially only making a tiny contribution to any policy changes as there will be other factors. Where you do have good relationships with the policy makers you can ask whether they are considering the findings/data you have provided when developing new policies, and what criteria are used in decision-making processes now.

The same applies for supply chains - in that sourcing items can be complex, but having the evidence of your complete supply chain provides consumers with confidence and demonstrates your impact. Supply Chain School[xlix] has a range of resources for how to measure the impact and sustainability of your supply chain. There is an increasing shift to full life cycle analysis of products and their impact – to inform consumers how much carbon, water and other resources have gone in to the production process – and how long they need to keep the product to offset that. Asket, a Swedish apparel brand introduced the Impact Receipt[1] – which shows the true cost of a garment's production (including CO_2 emissions, the amount of water used and energy consumption).

This is linked to the development of the circular economy and its eight Rs:

- Redesign
- Reduce
- Reuse
- Renew
- Repair
- Recycle
- Refuse
- Retrieve products to give them new uses or all of their possible uses

There are variations on what the 8Rs are, but if your organisation is trying to achieve any, or all, of these Rs then you will need to understand the current levels of each of these for your beneficiaries and track how this changes through the education, support or other help you provide. You can also do this at an organisational level – where you look at how businesses you support are implementing a circular economy.

If you are not an environmentally focused social enterprise, you still need to think about how your decisions affect the environment (either positively or negatively), including through:

- Waste reduction
- Buying local/ethical
- Carbon emissions
- Buying seasonal/non-seasonal food produce
- Plastic usage
- Your supply chain's environmental impact
- Travel
- Employing local/non-local people
- Using technology to reduce travel
- Water usage
- Recycling and reuse rates
- Pollution created
- Litter levels
- Impact on land, sea and species diversity of your activities
- Where you are sourcing materials from for your products
- The durability of your products versus frequent replacements
- Modern day slavery
- Policy change you achieve
- Campaigning and environmental activism

Nef has a good list of environmental indicators[li] for organisations to look at their energy usage, travel and commuting, waste and water. But, with many of the areas of environmental impact you will need to do some research in to your purchasing choices and your suppliers. As with social and community impacts, you do not need to measure every environmental impact you have to start with. You need to prioritise – typically this is by focusing on the areas where you know you have the biggest environmental impact. Then you can identify other areas in the future. The SDGs[xi] have a specific goal on sustainable consumption and production, so you could report against this goal.

A word on carbon offsetting and carbon neutral targets. Carbon offsetting is not something I believe is good. The reason for this is that it does not involve any behavioural change – as an organisation you can continue to consume and have a negative environmental impact because you offset your carbon. In reality, many of the carbon offsetting programmes never deliver the offsets. If you have carbon neutral targets for your organisation, make them a realistic (short) timescale, rather than in 20 years' time so you can start to implement change sooner, and report on your progress towards the targets annually. If you are looking to make comparisons between the carbon your product or manufacturing process creates versus other products/methods, there are a number of carbon calculators for different farming methods,[lii] different travel/transport methods[liii] and for different food choices[liv].

TECH IMPACT

Tech impact is about identifying the impact your technology usage has (through the technology you purchase such as computers, tablets, printers and phones, the frequency with which you replace them and your day-to-day data usage and energy consumption). There is an assumption that switching from face to face delivery to online reduces your carbon footprint. But the truth is using technology instead of travelling and delivering face-to-face still has a carbon footprint. Technology creates an environmental impact in a number of areas:

- The actual production process, shipping, usage and disposal of the technology you use (including the raw materials, energy and water usage)
- Your internet connected devices (for emails, audio calls and video calls, streaming films and videos, and gaming)
- Your data usage (either stored on your network or on the cloud)
- The volume of emails you send and receive
- Your usage of social media
- Usage of artificial intelligence (AI)

Digital data is a growing problem – as more people store data in the cloud – but this is still stored somewhere and it requires huge data centres. In 2016, the world's data centres used 3% of the global electricity supply and generated 2% of greenhouse gas emissions, which is the same as the aviation industry. By 2025, data will consume at least 20% of global electricity, and by 2040 the storage of digital data will create 14% of the world's emissions (the equivalent of the US's emissions now).[lv] It therefore, makes sense to try and reduce the amount of digital data we create and store.

Here are a few things you can do to identify and reduce your tech impact:

- Use your phones, tablets, printers and computer devices for longer before upgrading (using them for just six months longer offsets up to 40% of the emissions created during the product's production process)
- Recycle old equipment
- Use smaller devices to stream digital services (they use less energy)
- Use renewable energy sources to power and charge devices
- Only purchase what you need in terms of devices
- Buy your internet, webhosting and technology services from environmentally friendly suppliers
- Delete old emails (they are stored in a data centre)
- Do not send thank you emails or unnecessary emails
- Delete old files regularly (especially if you keep old versions of files)
- Unsubscribe from email newsletters and mailing lists that you do not read
- Only print when necessary
- Make traditional phone calls or audio only calls instead of video calls
- Reduce your time online and on social media (all that content you create is stored virtually)

If you are wondering why I said do not send thank you or unnecessary emails, data showed that on average people send 10 unnecessary emails every week (that is 520 per year), and if we each sent one less email per day it would be the equivalent of at least 43,260 flights from London to Madrid.[lvi]

There are not many tools you can use to measure your tech carbon footprint as most tend to focus on your overall personal carbon footprint. The WebCarbon Calculator[lvii] for digital footprint is very simple to use, and includes email, data transfer, streaming and web meeting calculators. You can use this now and again in six or 12 months' time to see if your tech footprint has changed. You can also switch to Ecosia[lviii] for searching online (they plant trees when you use their search engine). Tab for a Cause[lix] – which enables you to raise money for charity every time you open a new browser tab. Cleanfox[lx] enables you to unsubscribe from all those newsletters you no longer read easily. Greengeeks[lxi] provide green webhosting, as do Kualo[lxii].

Overall, with tech impact it is about taking small steps and regular actions on a daily basis, as these will contribute to reducing the environmental impact your technology usage has.

NEXT STEPS

Now that you have identified any areas of economic, environmental or tech impacts that you may want to measure, as well as how you will know the outcomes have been achieved, the following Chapter focuses on how you will collect the data.

CHAPTER 13: HOW WILL YOU COLLECT THE DATA?

O nce you have identified exactly how you will know your chosen outcomes have been achieved (and hopefully, the previous two Chapters on social, community, economic, environmental and tech impacts have given you several ideas), you then need to decide how you will collect the data. Most of you will use surveys, but there are other options available, which I will share here. Nowadays you can use most face-to-face methods online due to the vast number of apps available.

SURVEYS

Regardless of whether you physically see your stakeholders or not, surveys are still a very popular method for capturing impact data. You can create different types of surveys or questionnaires to gather the information you need. It's easiest to have a survey that you can use at the beginning and again at the end of the support or activities with the person (or after a certain time period such as three, six or 12 months) to track progress or change, rather than having two different surveys as making comparisons and tracking changes will be harder. If you are asking beneficiaries to complete surveys and self rank or score themselves it's best to use a simple Likert scale with four or five options. Use four options if you want to avoid people choosing the middle option – so they have an opinion one way or the other, and use five options if you want a middle option. Going beyond five options can make it difficult for people to make a choice between two options. It also tends to give you a cluster around the middle options and extremes, with no selection of the options inbetween. Depending on what you are asking in your questionnaire, these are the types of scales I tend to use:

- For agreeement or disagreement with a statement: Strongly disagree, Disagree, Agree, Strongly agree
- For frequency of an activity or action: Always, Very often, Sometimes, Rarely, Never
- For likeness to them: (Like me) To a Great Extent, Somewhat, Very Little, Not at All
- For importance of an item, area of support or action: Very important, Important, Moderately important, Of little importance, Unimportant

To make the collating and analyse stage easier, it is best to assign numbers to the options (e.g. strongly disagree is assigned 1, disagree 2, agree 3 and strongly agree 4). You will then be able to record the response as a numerical value – such as 2 (for disagree) when they complete the survey the first time, and 3 (for agree) when they complete it again. Then to identify the change subtract the numerical value for the most recent response from the earlier one (i.e. 3-2=1). This gives a value of one, showing a positive change/outcome. If the value is zero there is no change, and if it is a negative value, then the change/outcome is negative.

With scales its useful to have statements such as:

- Generally I feel positive about my future
- I have someone I can turn to for support
- I am usually a confident person
- I am able to cope with setbacks
- I am likely to re-offend in the next 3 months
- I am able to manage my money and budget
- I know how to self manage my illness

If you are going to create your own statements there are a few things to remember. First, be specific, but if you want to know how often someone does something or feels a particular way, ask them to think generally about the last two weeks, as otherwise they may look over a shorter or longer time period and think about specific events rather than their general circumstances or actions. Second, use statements that are worded positively and negatively to avoid people always selecting the same option. For example, I am usually confident when meeting new people could also be phrased as I am usually shy when meeting new people, rather than using negative words – and saying I am not confident whem meeting new people – as using not in the statements can confuse people (and lead to them selecting the opposite options to what they intended). Third, try not to make the survey too long or complicated, as you want to measure the right things – not everything. Finally, combine the use of your surveys with times when you will be asking your stakeholders for other information (such as during registration or a specific follow up session or email), so you are not sending them lots of different forms for completion.

If you do not physically see your stakeholders, and cannot do paperbased surveys, you can use various online survey tools[lxiii] or form builder apps[lxiv]. Survey Monkey is great if you have their email and also works well on mobile phones. Typeform allows you to add images/have a good design. Google Forms (Google's form builder that integrates with a spreadsheet) is straightforward to use. FreeOnlineSurveys creates a nice looking mobile phone version and has more question type options than the free versions of Typeform or Survey Monkey. YesInsights is for one click surveys – where you are being really lean and asking just one question. This would work well where you want to know what the priority is for a group or where you want to filter out people based on their response. You could then follow up with subsequent information or specific questions based on their response to the first question. If you need to get people to fill in the surveys when you are offline QuickTapSurvey allows you to download the survey to your phone/computer and then you can sync the survey responses to your account when you are online again. Survey Anyplace provides the option to gamify your survey – with a digital scratch card or digital slot machine – to offer the chance to win a prize if they complete the survey. For those of you that have lots of followers or have a Group on Facebook you can use Surveybot to create a chatbot survey via Messenger. Finally, if you want to take the stress out of designing your survey, SmartSurvey allows you to collaborate on the design by letting team members upload their questions, which can then be used to build the survey.

Other form builder tools (as well as Google Forms and Typeform are Microsoft Forms which collects results in Excel, Wufoo for creating quick graphical reports without spreadsheets (you choose the type of chart or graph you want to have the results displayed in – and this happens automatically without you needing to use a spreadsheet) and JotForm which you can customise more than Google Forms or Microsoft Forms – and they can be used for taking payments for bookings etc. Each of these survey builder tools or form builder apps has a free version that you can use – but if you need high response levels or need a specific type of question you may need to pay for that option. Also, many of these can be connected to Google Docs to automatically import responses to a spreadsheet, or this can be done using Zapier[lxv] to connect the survey to a document.

If you are testing or piloting your approach, you may wish to use a control group. The control group can then be compared to those that have participated in yor pilot to identify the effect of your activities. If you are looking to use control groups for surveys then I suggest you contact your local University to see if they are able to assist with the research, as they have access to a lot of datasets and could potentially undertake the research for you.

ALTERNATIVES TO SURVEYS

Surveys are not always the best way to capture data because some people find reading and/or writing difficult, or the questions are not worded in a user friendly way. In addition, there is limited engagement between you and the person completing the survey (unless you are helping them to complete it), and may people do not complete surveys (so your response rates could be low). This means surveys can often not be very inclusive. This section covers some alternative ways to capture your impact data.

Interviews

You could still use your survey questions, but you may need to design a different approach that will work with your stakeholder group, for example, through individual interviews. In 2017, I worked with an organisation that provided employability skills and work experience to young people with special educational needs. Most of the young people struggled with written communication and using questionnaires was not appropriate. The planned approach to data collection involved getting the teachers to have conversations with the young people about the work experience, starting with what they liked, what they didn't like, and moving to what they thought they had learnt and what they would like to do next.

This feedback was supported by further feedback from parents and the teachers – who shared what changes they had noticed in the young people. The work experience providers were also asked to share feedback on any changes in confidence, how they completed tasks during the work experience and how they communicated. This approach meant there was a range of different perspectives that highlighted the key outcomes and impacts for the young people.

Due to the way the questions were asked it enabled unintended outcomes to be captured as well. The organisation had expected the outcomes to be focused around employability skills (such as time keeping and knowing what a job involves), as well as soft outcomes including communication skills, confidence and hope/aspirations for the future. But what they found was that some of the young people had become confident travelling independently to their work experience placement (something they had never previously done) and had much more positive views about their futures and their potential opportunities, reflecting a new view of their learning difficulties as less of a barrier.

Online polls and live audience feedback apps

There are a number of online polls and live audience feedback apps[lxvi] you can use including Mentimeter, Poll Junkie, Easy Polls and Poll Everywhere (each of these has free options). These are great if you want to keep the audience engaged and develop the content based on the audience's responses, as well as tracking changes as a result of attending the event or activity. You share a link or ask people to download an app to their phone, to access the questions. They can be used either online or for face-to-face events/activities providing people can get online.

Washing line

The washing line is one of my favourite activities to do either face-to-face or virtually when you are running a group session. It is ideal if you want to get a snapshot of something before and after the session (such as confidence to do something, knowledge or skill levels). If you are face-to-face you use a piece of string with stickers with the numbers 1-10 on them along the string. You then give each person a peg. You can give everyone a different colour peg – or a peg with a number on it – if you want to track them individually, or you can give different groups different colour pegs (such as children having blue pegs and adults having red pegs) to track differences between these groups. Or you simply give out pegs to everyone randomly if you are happy to have an overall group response.

You ask each person to place their peg on the string at the number that represents their level of confidence at the start of the session – such as their confidence in measuring their organisation's impact. You add up the responses (e.g. three people placed their peg at number four, one at number six and another at number 7, gives a total score of 25 and an average of five), or record the individual responses if you are tracking each person. You then redo this at the end of the session and hopefully there has been a positive change in the score. I usually use one colour peg at the start (and leave these on the string) and another at the end, so the group can visually see their progression.

Baskets and balls or counters

These are ideal if you know people will not have much time to give you a response (for example, at a busy market or large event). You place a number of baskets or containers with numbers or smiley faces on them, and ask people to place a ball or counter in the basket/container that relates to their response. An example of this was an organisation that was trying to track how often their customers purchased their fruit and vegetables from the local market versus the supermarket. They had containers that said: Less than once a month, 2-3 times a month, Every week, More than once a week, Daily. For one week they asked about supermarkets and the following week about the local market, using the same possible responses on the containers. They totalled up the responses and then repeated the two questions again six months later to see if there were any changes in the frequency of purchasing from the local market.

Brick wall/graffiti wall

These are good activities – especially if you have used general questions, such as what has changed in your life since participating in this programme (see Chapter 11 for more information on these) – to get everyone sharing their responses. You can then group responses under themes and open up the conversation to get more detail around the themes (potentially putting people in to smaller groups or online breakout rooms). The brick wall activity involves either giving everyone a brick shaped piece of card and asking for a response to a particular question (with the brick added to a paper version of a wall). Or using an online brick wall template (you can design this in Google Jamboard or Miro – more on both of these shortly) and getting people to enter responses online. The graffiti wall is similar – except it is less organised as people simply add their comments to a large sheet of paper or interactive online whiteboard randomly. You then group the responses under themes together, and explore the changes in any key themes in more detail.

Dot voting

If you are trying to measure changes in knowledge and actions/behaviours, dot voting is a good activity. It can be completed individually or as a group activity, or used within a survey. Stickers are given to each person and they add them to the columns that apply to them on their sheet or the group sheet (see the example on the following page).

To track progression, dot voting needs to be done twice – the easiest way is to give the person stickers that are a different colour. You can then identify if people are implementing the information/knowledge you are sharing with them and making changes in their lives.

Item	I know about this	I have this or I do this
How to complete a CV	●	
Interview Skills	●	
Time keeping	●	●
Running a business		
Speaking confidently	●	

Equaliser

The Equaliser is great for scoring the change people want to see in their own life or the community. It needs to be completed twice to track what change happens, and can be done individually or in a group setting (where everyone scores it individually and an average is taken).

Item	Where it is now	Where you want it to be	At the end of this project (fill in at the end)
Community cohesion	3	8	
Crime	6	1	
Food poverty	7	1	
Activities for young people	2	9	

Interactive whiteboards

There are several good online interactive whiteboards[lxvii] available including Google Jamboard, Miro and Ideaboardz, as well as the one within Zoom. These are great for capturing feedback and data during online activities. The key thing is to build the data capture in to the activities so it happens naturally, rather than as something you expect people to do right at the end of the session.

Online diaries/journals, videos, audios and drawings

Where you are looking for people to reflect on their progress, online diaries are a good option, such as Diarium (which is available to download from Google Play or the App Store). The online versions allow people to include audio, photos, videos and music as well as text. I have seen this used successfully with young people. If you are working with small numbers of people you can use videos, audios or drawings to capture impact. You would ask them to record a short piece of audio or a video answering a question, or produce a drawing that represents their answer to the question. Audio works well with dementia patients – as you can replay what they said previously to trigger other thoughts. Providing you have their permission, you can create a montage of the video clips to share your impact findings. As they are individual diaries, audios, videos or drawings they will take time to analyse, but if you ask them to answer specific questions it makes that process easier (and also ensures they provide you with information about the outcomes and impact you are measuring).

OTHER CONSIDERATIONS

There are two other things to consider in relation to how you will collect the data. The first is when (how often) – which will be based on if you are doing your data capture retrospectively or planning to do the impact measurement before you start delivery. Ideally, you will want before and after data to make an accurate comparison in order to assess which outcomes have been achieved. If there's no "before" data, then it will need to be done retrospectively, where stakeholders are asked to reflect back on what life was like before (although this is not as accurate as collecting the details of their current circumstances at the beginning of working with them). If you don't have beneficiaries then you will need to think what before and after is – is there a way to assess it currently and again later? For example, for business growth, you could measure their income and profit levels now and in a year's time.

The second is what demographic data do you need as part of the collection process. This will assist you with analysing your data (as you will be able to identify if particular sub-groups experience different levels of change to others). You may decide to capture information as part of the registration process such as age, employment status, health conditions, ethnicity etc. but whatever you decide to capture make sure it is necessary, otherwise you are in breach of the data protection regulations.

NEXT STEPS

You have now completed the Plan stage. The next step is to get on with doing the data collection – in the Measure stage.

Chapter 14: Measure

N
ow you have worked through the Plan stage and have everything prepared (by knowing what you want to measure, how you will evidence the change has happened and how you will capture the data) then the Measure stage is straightforward. This is when you physically start to capture your impact data – because you can now be confident that everything is in place for you to do this well.

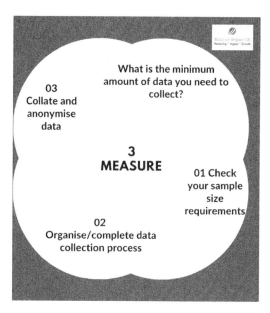

As with the previous stages, this stage focuses on three areas:

1. Check your sample size
2. Organise and complete your data collection process
3. Collate and anonymise your data

First off – remember this approach looks at the minimum viable amount of data collection that enables you to test if you are achieving your ultimate goal or not. Therefore, it is best to check the sample size you need to have enough valid data. You can do this using a Sample Size Calculator[lxviii]. Generally, the smaller your group the more people you need to consult to make sure the data is valid; this will give you a target in terms of the number of responses you will need.

Then start the collection phase. This is where you will need to be organised to make sure the collection actually happens. One of the cross-cutting themes (embedding) is vital during this stage. Your data collection processes need to sit within the existing bricks of your organisation and not be additional rows of bricks on top of the existing ones. The other analogy I use here is for you to imagine that collecting impact data has been sprinkled over everyone in the organisation like glitter, so each person has a small (but vital) role to play in your impact data collection. Whilst one person may be accountable for making sure the data is collected, the responsibility for it should sit with several people.

To achieve this think about every single contact point you have with your chosen stakeholder groups (e.g. face to face, via email, phone calls, sales/purchase emails etc.) and how you could incorporate data collection in to your existing activities and processes. You should have a maximum of four outcomes you are measuring (two for each stakeholder group, plus a potential further question asking about any other outcomes, and then a few bits of data on the person's demographics).

You can then identify who is best placed to capture the data and when. Make sure they understand why you are collecting the data and what needs completing or doing. Then check in after a couple of weeks to see if the data is being collected. This might sound obvious, but if things are going to go wrong with your impact measurement it will be here with people not doing any data collection. It is a good idea to check with those capturing the data and ask for feedback, so you know if you need to make any changes to how you ask the questions or how you collect the data.

Finally, make sure you collate the data. The easiest way to do this is in a simple spreadsheet, where you record the responses, so you can look at the data for your whole stakeholder group. If you are using online surveys you can automatically send the data to a spreadsheet. Hopefully, you have used numerical values for any scales you are using (see the section on Surveys in Chapter 13) so the values are automatically imported in to the spreadsheet. If not, now is the time to assign values to the scales/options for any questions of this type, so you record the responses as numerical values. This will make the Analyse stage easier. If you are using methods that require someone to write up the key themes and areas (such as journals) then make sure this happens. It is crucial that any impact data is collated as soon as possible so any issues can be flagged up at the earliest opportunity.

And that is it! The Measure stage really is the simplest one (providing you have done the work in the Plan stage).

NEXT STEPS

Once you have collected your data it is time to move on to the Analyse stage, and see what your impact data is telling you.

SECTION THREE: MANAGING IMPACT

CHAPTER 15: ANALYSE

The Analyse stage is one of the best stages, as you get to find out what your impact data is telling you. It is where you find out whether your current efforts are bringing you closer to your ultimate goal or not, and can start to manage your impact. You might be a bit nervous about doing any analysis as the result could go either way. However, it is the only way to know for sure.

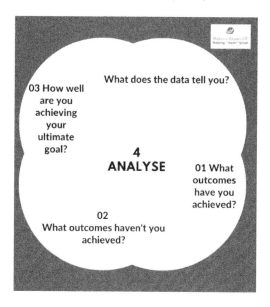

The Analyse stage is something I encourage you to do on a regular basis. Take a look at the data as you capture it so you do not miss any important feedback, or changes in outcomes. That ways you can make immediate changes to your delivery as required. Keep the Analyse stage manageable by building it in to your existing processes and activities. You can do this by:

- Identifying who will be responsible for completing the initial analysis
- How often you will analyse the data
- Where you will record and keep the findings of your initial analysis
- When the data will be shared and discussed (e.g. at team meetings)
- Who will be responsible for making any changes to the data collection processes and the delivery if required

Once you have agreed the process for the Analyse stage, there are three key questions to focus on to find out what the data is telling you:

1. What outcomes have you achieved?
2. What outcomes haven't you achieved?
3. How well are you achieving your ultimate goal?

The first two questions are straightforward. You will be looking for what changes your stakeholders have and have not achieved. This will mostly likely involve comparing before and after responses from surveys or your other data collection methods. If you used scales for questions then you can simply compare the numerical values for the responses in the two surveys, and identify positive outcomes (positive numerical values), negative outcomes (negative numerical values) and no outcomes (zero numerical value). For other types of data collection you will need to identify key words/themes. You could use a key word extractor app but these may miss the context in which the key words are used. This is why it is important to limit the outcomes you choose to measure and number of questions you ask, otherwise the Analyse stage becomes a huge, time-consuming job.

The next steps are then:

- Count the positive and negative outcomes you have achieved, as well as those with no change (taking care not to aggregate the data – so you end up with an average that ignores the negative outcomes)
- Explore and identify reasons for what went well, what needs improving and what needs changing
- Look for patterns regarding who experiences change and who does not
- Create charts and tables to display the data in a summary

Some useful follow-up questions to consider at this point are:

- Did you expect to achieve particular outcomes and have now found out that you do not achieve them? If so, why is that?
- Are there any unintended outcomes (positive or negative) that stakeholders have told you about?
- Do certain stakeholder characteristics affect the types of outcomes they achieve (e.g. age, health, geographical location, gender)?

You may also decide to undertake a cost-benefit analysis or Social Return on Investment (SROI) calculation as part of your analysis. This is covered in Chapter 16.

The Analyse stage is really a short, sharp and focused quick dive in to what your data is telling you – so you can identify any obvious issues quickly and remedy them straightaway. It is not the same as the Learn stage – which focuses on the learnings from your data and how you can seek to maximise your impact (more on this in Chapter 17).

Answering these questions, and regularly completing your analysis, will help you come to an organic understanding to answer the final question: How well are you achieving your ultimate goal? This is linking you back to the beginning (where you defined your ultimate goal and created a theory of change). If the Analyse stage seems like a lot of questioning, trust me on this, you need to explore your data in order to be confident that your activities are delivering the change you intend to achieve.

NEXT STEPS

Now you have completed the initially phase of the management part of IMM, it is time to shift your focus to strategic management of your impact – with the Learn stage of the approach in Chapter 17. Alternatively, look at monetising your outcomes using SROI in Chapter 16, before moving on to the Learn stage.

CHAPTER 16: SOCIAL RETURN ON INVESTMENT (SROI)

W hen you come to the Analyse stage you may decide that you want to add financial values (proxies) to the outcomes you have achieved or to calculate the SROI you have delivered. SROI is a type of cost benefit analysis. This Chapter provides an overview of the steps involved in valuing your outcomes and turning your impact data in to an SROI figure.

SROI is most useful if you are trying to calculate the potential monetary savings from your intervention, such as for a public sector body. This is because there are a lot of different financial proxies that are readily available[lxix] for the potential fiscal savings such as the costs of treating different health conditions, adult day care services, employment, education and training, social services, criminal activities and housing. Some financial proxies provide the economic and social values for the outcomes individuals have achieved. It is more difficult to find values for soft outcomes (although the Value Game[lxx] is covered later in this Chapter as an option for obtaining values for these).

For hard outcomes, such as employment, financial proxies are used and are easier to calculate. This is because there is a monetary value for the wages the individual receives as well as any benefits they no longer receive. To assign monetary values to your outcomes, you have a choice of three different types of financial proxies:

- The cost of negative outcomes avoided, e.g. medical costs avoided, benefit costs avoided
- Actual spending on similar outcomes, e.g. the cost of improving confidence by attending a confidence course
- People's Willingness to Pay which asks people to hypothetically assign a value to an outcome, e.g. how much an individual would be willing to pay for improved wellbeing

You can use financial values (proxies) without doing a full SROI calculation. For example, if you support individuals who are on benefits in the UK to get a job, you can use a figure of c.£19,000[lxxi] as the total public value (which includes fiscal savings to the government and the economic benefit to the individual). There is no need to go further and do a full SROI. However, to avoid overstating the financial values, you cannot claim that the full ££19,000 is 100% due to your organisation's work. To overcome this issue, when using financial values, I recommend you state that these are the known fiscal/economic values for the outcomes you have contributed to (rather than you have achieved).

You can also use SROI as a performance metric to support investment and operational decision-making. More details of how this can be done are provided in Chapter 18 on impact metrics.

DATA REQUIRED FOR SROI

To calculate your SROI you will need to collect some additional data to make your calculations as robust as possible:

- Financial values for the inputs (staff time, money etc. that was needed to deliver your outcomes)
- Total number of activities delivered and people/organisations/businesses supported
- Your outcome figures for your project/organisation
- If you're including your organisation's economic and/or environmental impact in the scope of your SROI calculations you will need data on new jobs created, volunteering opportunities, training provided to staff, carbon emissions, waste to landfill etc.
- The values for the adjustments (see below)

THE ADJUSTMENTS

SROI is calculated for the impact you have. The value reflects the proportion of the outcomes you can claim as a result of the activities you have delivered. In order to do this various adjustments are made to the values assigned to the outcomes:

- Deadweight – this represents the number of outcomes that would have been achieved anyway without your activities.
- Attribution – this is an adjustment for the contribution of other agencies to the achievement of your outcomes.

- Drop off – this is an adjustment for outcomes that will not be sustained.
- Displacement – this is an adjustment for other activities that have been displaced as a result of the activities you deliver.

To obtain values for these adjustments you need to collect additional information from your stakeholders. The easiest ways to do this are to ask the following questions:

Deadweight: How much do you think we have contributed to the changes that you have achieved? Use percentages (0-20, 21-40, 41-60, 61-80, 81-100), and then obtain an average percentage for the stakeholder group.

Attribution: Have you received support from any other organisations or individuals, which has helped you to achieve the changes in your life? (Yes/No). Then calculate a percentage for those saying Yes. You can be more specific about 'changes in your life' so it is relevant to your activities.

Drop off: This will require you to do a follow up after the activity or support has been completed (ideally at 12 months) to see if the outcome is still sustained. Then calculate a percentage for those that have not sustained an outcome.

Displacement: If you had not received the support from us, would you have gone elsewhere? (Yes/No). Then calculate a percentage for those saying Yes to identify your displacement percentage.

Each of these adjustments is applied as a percentage reduction to the financial proxy. For example, if your financial proxy was £2,000; and your deadweight, attribution, drop off and displacement were each 15% (60% in total), then you would reduce the value as follows: £2000 X (100%-60%) to give a revised value of £800. This value is then multiplied by the number of times that outcome has been achieved. Finally, the total value is divided by the total cost to give a value of £xx for every £1 spent on delivery.

In most cases, outcomes are typically based on the current year and a further one-year period, as the impact of an activity tends to reduce significantly after one further year, and to continue to claim for an outcome beyond this period could result in over claiming. Although, where you are delivering over a long time period and tracking your beneficiaries it would be possible to calculate over that period (such as for an eating disorder service that tracked individuals for 10 years to confirm the outcomes were sustained). For the calculations this involves applying the drop off rate in each subsequent year.

THE VALUE GAME

The Value Game[lxxii] is a survey tool that helps you to prioritise and put values to outcomes, and is particularly useful for soft outcomes or outcomes where there are no existing financial proxies. It shows how the stakeholder group value the outcomes relative to other products they also value. It costs Euro180 annually to have access to the Value Game. You can make each game specific to your stakeholder group (by including products that are of value to them). You then send it directly to them via email or via a web link so they can participate, or alternatively you can run it as a group activity during a face-to-face or virtual session. I have seen this used very effectively with a group of young people to value an increase in positivity, and the products used included designer clothes, trainers, phones and other tech gadgets. The only potential downside to using things like the Value Game is that valuations from stakeholders tend to be higher than those from literature or other research sources.

OTHER CONSIDERATIONS WITH SROI

If you take your SROI to the basics, there are only two numbers to change – the value of your impact (which is based on the financial values you have used and the amount of adjustment you have made to these), and the costs you included for delivering your activities. Using the biggest values and the smallest costs will give you a bigger SROI value, and means that SROI is open to manipulation.

Each organisation preparing a SROI uses their own valuations, as there are no accepted conventions for valuing outcomes – although there is increasing standardisation of values. When deciding upon the values to use within SROI you should make sure you are not using the highest valuations available unless these are justified. As you can choose different valuations, SROI ratios cannot be compared, and the case studies and other information become equally important in providing evidence of the effectiveness of your organisation or project.

To avoid over claiming, only include outcomes that have been verified through data that you collected and the same with your adjustments. Don't understate the adjustments (or say it is zero unless you have proof that it is), and if you are unable to get percentages for the adjustments look at what similar organisations have included in their SROI reports. Never overstate your SROI or the financial savings – so please only talk about 'potential' savings to the public sector – as in reality the budget would be used elsewhere so there will be no real savings. Having an SROI of £100 for every £1 you spend on delivery does not look credible.

Another consideration is double counting of individuals and their outcomes. This is a particular issue if you are measuring several different outcomes. In those cases you would identify the main outcome achieved and value that. Similarly, you need to adjust for unintended and negative outcomes (these should be picked up through your impact data collection processes). It is common for some areas of activity to need adjusting negatively – such as where the value of the outcome is lower than the cost of delivery, or where alongside the positive outcomes there are negative ones as well.

As well as an evaluative SROI you can also do predictive SROI calculations. These are useful if you are tendering or applying for funding and want to include a monetary value for your impact, or to estimate the total potential savings from your intervention. The predictive SROI can be used as a monitoring tool to check you are on track with your outcomes and impact delivery (in a similar way to a budget versus actual financial forecast).

NEXT STEPS

If you are interested in completing a SROI calculation for your organisation I recommend you look at the comprehensive resources that Social Value UK[lxxiii] and Social Value International[lxxiv] provide.

CHAPTER 17: LEARN

You've made it to stage five – Learn! This is the impact management stage of the approach where you focus on what you are going to do to continually improve and refine your impact.

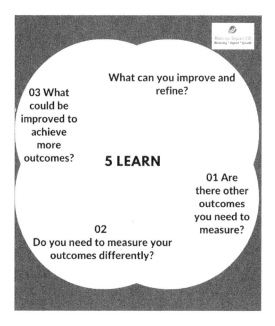

As with the other stages there are three questions to help you focus:

1. Are there other outcomes you need to measure?
2. Do you need to measure your outcomes differently?
3. What could be improved to achieve more outcomes?

This stage does not happen as frequently as stage four (Analyse). Usually Learn fits in with your business planning processes, and is something you look at annually or half yearly. It is about putting a strategic lens to your IMM and being forward looking, rather than the more short-term reactionary approach that the Analyse stage provides.

This stage includes a focus on making your impact measurement processes better. You will be learning about what matters to your stakeholders – what outcomes do they want to achieve and have you collected enough information on these to evidence that they have happened? If not, go back to stage one and two to define and plan what outcomes you want to measure and what data you want to collect based on what you have learnt this time. You may find other outcomes that matter more to your stakeholders and decide to start measuring these outcomes instead, or in addition, to the ones you are already measuring. Also, consider if you need to measure outcomes for other stakeholder groups in future.

If you struggled to capture data you may need to rethink how you gather the data, and try a different method. For example, if you tried surveys and did not get many responses, you may now decide to use a graffiti wall. The other aspect of this question is about the design of the questions/statements you use – and these may not have worked as intended, and you may decide to reword them or completely change them.

The third question takes a deeper look at the data and feedback to identify patterns and to support what you'll do going forward, either by changing what you deliver or developing new elements (or products or services) to reduce any negative or unintended outcomes you delivered, and to increase your positive impacts. This question is about proactively managing the changes that are most important to your stakeholders, so you can maximise your impact.

You should report back to your stakeholders with this information, and share what you are going to do to reduce your negative or unintended outcomes. In addition, report on any changes you will be making to the way you deliver your activities based on the impact data you have received.

This stage supports your business planning processes and will help to develop your strategy going forward – as you may identify gaps in your products/services that you want to address, or where you want to partner with another organisation to make sure your clients get the support they need, or to develop a new aspect of your delivery. You may have identified particular barriers or issues that segments of your stakeholders have during the Analyse stage, that result in you developing new activities to address these and improve their outcomes.

There are three possible results from this stage (and I have experienced all of these with organisations I have worked with):

When you completed stage four you found you were achieving the ultimate goal and outcomes you desired – and now the learning for you is how can you improve those outcomes further, and what else could you measure? An organisation I worked with, decided after the first year of impact measurement, which had focused on hard outcomes around employment and training, to capture more data on soft outcomes the second year. This made sense as they actually achieved more soft outcomes than hard outcomes, but without the data could not prove it. They focused on measuring changes in confidence and aspirations for the future, as well as mental health and wellbeing.

Or at stage four you found out you were not achieving your ultimate goal, or the outcomes you intended, then it's a case of needing to revisit what you are doing based on this information to improve things and refine your product/service/delivery so it achieves what you intended. Again, with an organisation that delivered counselling services their impact data showed that they were not achieving any improvements in family relationships for their beneficiaries – although there were positive changes in anxiety levels these were not reflected in the family relationships. So they decided to focus on providing additional support to the beneficiaries alongside their family members.

Or, worst case scenario, it's time to realise what you are doing is not going to work and deliver the impact you had hoped for. You can either decide to work towards a different ultimate goal and outcomes based on what you have learnt or you can decide to stop – as you have realised that what you are doing is not going to work and it is no longer something you want to pursue. This actually happens a lot – many organisations are testing a model of delivery only to find it is not that impactful. I have seen this with organisations that try to work in isolation on one issue with young people, which does not take in to account the causality and interconnectedness of other areas of the person's life. The same applies to many of the regeneration programmes that have been delivered in the UK (where poverty levels remain the same in those communities) because the underlying issues were not addressed.

And that's how the fifth stage of Lean Social Impact Approach takes you neatly back to the first stage (Define) where you revisit your ultimate goal, develop an impact led strategy that will achieve that goal and Plan, Measure and Analyse the outcomes that help you achieve that ultimate goal.

By learning in this way you enter a cycle of continually improving your impact and outcomes. Rather than looking at the Lean Social Impact Approach as a process of measuring impact for the sake of it, it becomes about managing the impact you have. This is achieved by collecting the right data and using that data to guide and direct your work so that you can continually enhance and maximise the impact you have.

NEXT STEPS

Now you've completed the Lean Social Impact Approach it is time to share your impact data with others. In the next two Chapters I will be focusing on impact metrics and Board reporting, and Sharing your impact findings.

CHAPTER 18: IMPACT METRICS

Very often once all the hard work of collecting and analysing impact data is done, a glossy marketing report is created and nothing else happens. In this Chapter, you will be focusing on sharing your impact data internally, and what good impact metrics are for your staff team and Board reporting. I will also share how SROI can be used as a performance metric to support decision-making.

If you have successfully implemented the three cross cutting themes you will hopefully be sharing impact findings and data already. Although focused on impact investors, a great resource for exploring the types of metrics to use for continual improvement is The GIIN's "The Business Value of Impact Measurement"[lxxv] which highlights five areas where organisations can derive value from measuring their impact:

- Revenue growth (by refining and developing products and services, identifying new markets or customer segments, better understanding how to market and communicate to customers)
- Operational effectiveness and efficiency (focused on improving processes and systems)
- Investment decisions (what to invest in)

- Marketing and reputation building (building trust with potential customers)
- Strategic alignment and risk mitigation (checking you are in alignment with your overall purpose and making changes as required).

But what do good impact metrics look like for staff teams and Boards?

FOR STAFF TEAMS

Good impact metrics for staff teams enable an on-going focus on impact and effective operational decision-making. That means impact data must be up to date, regularly available and presented in an easy to understand format.

For each of your areas of delivery the manager should have access to metrics that are shared with the rest of the team. This may include a target for when outcomes are flagged up for further review (if they are below a certain level). It should also include a comparison with your equality and diversity data to flag any issues in accessibility, design or delivery of your activities. Finally, the impact data you share needs to link back to your organisational purpose and ultimate goal, so there is always clarity around why any changes are being made to operational activities. Impact should be a regular item for team meetings, with updates and training provided to staff on IMM either during team meetings or at separate sessions.

Any major issues need to be shared at more senior team meetings (if you have separate delivery team meetings) – so that other areas of your organisation are aware of what is happening, and any common organisational wide issues can be identified and addressed.

FOR BOARDS

Boards are either inundated with too much impact data or none at all. Many Boards choose to focus on financial information at their meetings, accompanied by an Operational Review that does not include any impact data. But getting the balance right between financial and impact data is crucial. One without the other is not telling the full story of your organisation's position. I recommend reporting your impact data on no more than two pages and covering four key areas. This needs to include:

- Your outcomes success rate – the levels of outcomes against what you planned to deliver (basically a budget versus actual for outcomes)
- Any activities where outcomes are below an agreed level (I like using traffic lights – so activities that are of concern would be red, amber for those that are achieving in some areas and not in others, and green for activities that are achieving their targets)
- Further commentary on any activities that are highlighted as red and the actions being taken to remedy this
- One or two environmental key performance indicators – KPIs (such as carbon footprint, tech

impact or waste data) so that you can assess how well through your operations you are minimising your impact on the environment

You could also calculate the cost per outcome (this KPI would need to be developed based on what is relevant for your own organisation, and only used where it is easy to assign costs to particular outcomes).

Reporting to the Board really does not need to include anything more. Too often Boards are not operating at a strategic level, as they try to get involved in operational decisions. Providing the Board has information to show that any areas of concern are being addressed, they do not need to get involved in how these issues are addressed.

Then annually the Board and staff team need to have a strategy session to review the ultimate goal of the organisation – to ensure it is still appropriate. This strategy session will include a discussion of the learnings from stage five of the approach to support you to develop new activities and to identify activities you need to stop doing.

SROI As A Performance Metric

SROI can be part of your decision-making processes at both operational and strategic levels. For Boards that are frequently faced with decisions between conflicting investment options or business options, it makes sense to base your decision on more than just financial data. Plus when you are carrying out your day-to-day operational activities SROI can be used to monitor performance and to identify areas for improvement.

Just like the Balanced Scorecard,[lxxvi] which includes non-financial elements alongside financial, to provide a performance measurement system, using an SROI based performance metric is no use on its own – otherwise your decisions would simply be based on the option that provides the highest SROI value for every £1 spent. To incorporate SROI in a performance metric requires a balance of different elements. This includes:

Financial data (i.e. what are the financial returns for this investment/new product or service; when will break even be reached; what kind of initial investment is needed; what are the cash-flow implications; how risky is this etc.). This will enable your organisation to consider the resources required and the financial return that will be generated for each option.

Operational data (i.e. how easily can you implement this; what training is required; what are the operational risks etc.). This is really looking at how different this option is from what your organisation currently does, and how quickly your organisation could mobilise to start delivering and having an impact.

Social impact data through SROI (i.e. what social value does this investment decision create; what social return is achieved for every £1; who does the social value get generated for – local people, the local economy, the environment or local statutory and public sector agencies etc.). This enables stakeholders to be involved in the decision-making processes – by asking them what outcomes matter to them so your organisation can generate more social value.

As well as using SROI for your investment decisions, SROI can also be an operational KPI to ensure your organisation is delivering what it plans, monitoring over or under achievement against particular outcomes, and to embed a culture of continuous improvement by striving to improve the SROI.

NEXT STEPS

This Chapter has covered how you can share your impact data and metrics internally to support decision-making. The following Chapter focuses on sharing your impact findings externally with your stakeholders.

CHAPTER 19: SHARING YOUR IMPACT FINDINGS

This is the bit everyone loves – creating a glossy marketing impact report – where you celebrate all the successes and ignore all the things that haven't gone so well. Sadly, that is not how to go about sharing your impact findings. You also do not need to create a report – especially not a huge impact report in many cases (unless you really want to or have to for a funder). Let's bust that myth straight away! The main reason for not doing this is that no-one reads them from cover to cover – so all your time will be wasted.

When it comes to sharing your impact findings, here are a few things to bear in mind:

- Be really clear about who you are sharing your impact findings with – and what they will be interested in knowing
- Decide what format is best for the audience you are targeting (report, audio, video, interactive graphics, infographic etc.)
- Be honest and transparent – share details of how you have measured your impact, areas where you have not measured anything, and how confident

you are that the impact that has been achieved
results from your activities

- Do not be afraid to share your negative or
  unintended outcomes. Include what you are going
  to do to minimise these going forward

WHAT MAKES A GOOD IMPACT REPORT?

This is possibly a million dollar question, as I do not
believe there is just one answer. Below I share what I
consider makes a good impact report. An Impact Report
is not a list of numbers of people who have attended
events, visited your centre or engaged in an activity,
alongside lots of pictures of people smiling and having
fun. That is simply the outputs you have achieved – and
not your impact.

An Impact Report details the difference you have made to
people and the planet, and your organisation's social,
community, economic, tech and environmental impacts as
appropriate. It may or may not include case studies and
feedback, but the best Impact Reports combine facts and
figures about your impact with the personal stories of
your beneficiaries/clients.

Some commonalities between good impact reports are:

- Brand consistency (colours, tone etc.)
- Clearly describe what their organisation is trying
  to achieve in terms of impact
- Use photos/images and graphics well to highlight
  key points and bring the data to life

- Include qualitative and quantitative data (case studies/feedback/quotes alongside figures)
- Do not cram too much information or data in – they stick to the key messages and points throughout
- Have a strong summary at the start of the report (so you want to read more)
- Are no more than 12 pages long, and each page is not overloaded with text
- Detail their methodology (how their impact data has been collected) and what they want to improve or do differently in the future

To create a good impact report you need to be clear on your impact story – the consistent thread that goes through all of your work and impact. This may be presented from a different angle depending on who the audience is (e.g. if your audience is the public sector you might consistently focus on and talk about the economic impacts of your activities, whereas if it is funders you might talk more about the social impacts). There are links to a few examples of reports here[lxxvii], including a video and infographic format for reporting. If you think you cannot create something that looks like this, you can start by planning and writing your content (one theme/activity per page, with a summary page and a contact us page). Then choose a template in Canva[lxxviii] and switch it to your brand colours. Finally add charts or other icons and any photos you have.

Alternative Ways To Share Your Impact Findings

If you do not want to create an Impact Report here are a number of alternative ways to share your impact findings. The key thing with any content is to repurpose it – so have a consistent way of creating content so that case studies can be used as standalone items as well as being part of a report, or turned in to a video, social media post etc.

Videos

Videos are a really accessible way to share your impact findings. They need to be around 2.5-3 minutes long. Any longer and they are unlikely to get watched all the way through. The format for a video is as follows:

- The Founder/CEO shares why your organisation exists and the impact you're trying to create
- A beneficiary shares their story - What was life like before, what activities/support have they accessed and what changes has that helped them to achieve/what is life like now
- The Founder/CEO comes back on to share the overall impact figures for that activity or your whole organisation

If you are new to video creation and do not want to record yourself/others speaking to camera, you can create a video using text and images. By using Lumen5[lxxix] you can do this quickly by simply pasting text on their site (although you will probably want to swap or change some of the images it pre-selects as being relevant to the video's content with your own images or ones from their library). The videos on Lumen5 will include the key parts of the text you pasted in. Alternatively, you can create an animated video using Powtoon[lxxx] - these are particularly useful if you want to explain key points or share facts and figures. To make sure your videos are accessible include subtitles – these can be added via YouTube using their automated captioning (but you do need to check they are correct).

Case Studies

Case studies tell a client's story and are supported by facts and figures for that particular service. The format for a case study follows the middle section of the video format about. You can ask the individual the three questions and record the audio, and then write up the case study afterwards. You need to get their approval to share it, and permission to use their name etc. If you are anonymising the case study make sure there is no information that would enable them to be re-identified (such as them being the only person with a particular health condition). A strong case study will have one or two quotes from the client included, as well as a summary of that service (numbers supported, outcomes achieved and any financial values you wish to include).

Infographics

Infographics are basically fancy charts and graphs that can be used for social media posts to highlight key figures/pieces of information. You can link them back to your website for more detailed information on that area of delivery or a particular area of impact. You can also include infographics in your Impact Report. Canva[lxxviii] has free infographic templates that you can customise. There are some infographic examples here[lxxxi] – although not all of these examples are impact infographics, (some are explaining why their organisation is needed and the problem they are trying to solve) – they are good examples of how to communicate facts in a simple way.

Interactive images and virtual tours

Thinglink[lxxxii] is an online app that can be used to create user-led interactive experiences. This is one of the few paid tools I recommend people use ($25 per month), as it is simple to use and effective. You can create engaging content that can be embedded on your website. The user can click on icons to read more about the areas of your impact of interest to them. This can include maps – showing your delivery locations – or an image that then has links to case studies, videos, audio or text.

Podcasts

Podcasts are a great way to share a client's journey and to talk in detail about your impact – ideally with you and your client on the podcast together. You can either create your own podcast audio (and upload it to your website) or be a guest on another existing podcast show. If you are creating your own podcasts, decide on the structure and the questions you plan to ask so the client is prepared.

Photo gallery/wall or graffiti wall

As well as being a good way to capture impact data, a photo gallery/wall or graffiti wall are great ways to share what you actually did and include your clients and other stakeholders' feedback. Ideally, the feedback will be about the impact of your organisation rather than about what they liked/did not like about the activities.

Stakeholder events

You can engage your stakeholders via an event (online or offline) to share your impact findings. These are useful when you want to talk about your plans for the future – in particular how you're planning to continually improve or further develop your activities to maximise your impact. You can also do stakeholder panels where you have a funder, partner organisation, beneficiary and staff member on the panel, and someone asks them questions to share the impact your organisation has had. These are ideal if you have potential funders, commissioners and investors in the audience.

NEXT STEPS

Have fun sharing your impact findings with others, and if you want please share them with me. I love learning about your social enterprises, and seeing how creatively you share your impact findings.

CHAPTER 20: THE FUTURE

This book would not be complete without a bit of future gazing! So, here are my predictions on the future of impact measurement and management.

We will see IMM increasingly align to the SDGs. This one does not involve much predictive abilities as we are already seeing this happen through the SDG Impact Standards[lxxxiii] (with standards for Private Equity Funds, Bonds and Enterprises). These standards are focused on four areas (Strategy, Management Approach, Governance and Transparency) and are more about the systems and processes that you can use to manage your contribution to the SDGs rather than how well you perform against the SDGs.

However, I believe that there will be an increasing alignment between the SDGs and what is measured through impact measurement, particularly as we get ever closer to the 2030 deadline for achieving the SDGs. The Impact Management Project[lxxxiv] is focused on getting global consensus around how impact is measured, managed and reported – so I do not doubt this standardisation will happen. This includes alignment with GRI (Global Reporting Initiative) standards[lxxxv] and other global standards too.

But let's not go too crazy about standardisation – because it would not be relevant for every organisation – and the SDGs don't cover every possible outcome organisations may be delivering. I do believe there will be more niche impact measurement tools appearing over the coming years – that have been co-designed with the stakeholders, and pull in the value of lived experience in terms of how you measure the impact of your activities.

This leads me nicely on to Doughnut Economics[lxxxvi] - an approach and way of thinking that acknowledges that the economy only functions properly when it is aligned with society and the planet, and organisations seek to contribute rather than extract profits and resources from the planet. I suggest you read the book by Kate Raworth to learn more about this, because I cannot do justice to it in one paragraph. The Doughnut is being used for place-based programmes, to seek a holistic approach. I believe it will be used by more organisations to identify the interconnectedness of their outcomes in communities, and to make sure sections of the community are not left behind, especially around food, housing, health and poverty. It will also be used to hold businesses to account for their environmental impact on local communities.

Having a positive environmental and tech impact will lead to a growth in the circular economy and being carbon negative. Organisations will try to assess the impact of their supply chain and their own environmental and tech policies, to prove they are not damaging the environment. Not all of this will be genuine, and I anticipate some more "impact washing" over the next few years. We will see more apps and tools available to conduct full life cycle analysis of products and blockchain style apps being used to verify the credentials of supply chains. Alongside this, globally there will be more countries implementing social procurement policies for public sector spending, and with that a resulting increase in large corporations and businesses attempting to measure their impact. There will not be much impact management by these corporations – as it will simply be a case of measuring their impact to win contracts and tenders.

CHAPTER 21: IMM IN TIMES OF CHANGE AND CRISIS

Following 2020, when it comes to your IMM it is vital that you're prepared for the unexpected. This final Chapter gives you some tips for when you are having to change your delivery methods and/or activities during a crisis, but still want to know if you are achieving impact.

In short, it is about doing what you can with what you have available (pretty much the Lean Social Impact Approach but slimmed down even further). The reasoning when looking at IMM in a crisis is that some things simply will not be worth your time measuring because you will be focused on crisis management and actual delivery.

IMM can help you during a crisis, and that is why it is a good idea to still collect some data anyway. Firstly, it can help you decide what to stop, start, pause or continue doing because it makes you lead with impact first and gives you a focus (rather than just jumping from one activity to another without an impact-led strategy). It does not make sense to go from mentoring people to making food – you have got no knowledge of food hygiene etc. and you are probably not best placed to deliver it, even if there is demand for that service.

You are better off focusing your energy on what you can adapt of what you previously did, and thinking how you will adapt post-crisis. To do this, think about how you can best meet the needs of people and the planet, and create impact that is in alignment with your organisational purpose. To make it easy for you to work through whatever delivery you are doing now and what you are thinking about doing in the future, there are five steps to help you:

1. Identify the problem
2. Prioritise the outcomes
3. Get feedback
4. Adapt
5. Make decisions

Identify the problem

Initially, to identify the problem, there are two questions to ask yourself:

One is what is the problem we are trying to solve?

And, two, how can we maximise the impact we have?

Yes, you do need to go back to these questions – because a crisis will in many cases have changed the problem for your beneficiaries as they prioritise their immediate needs such as:

- Food
- Shelter
- Health and wellbeing

- Paying their bills
- Accessing support with their finances
- Support to combat social isolation

By answering these two questions, you will be able to see what you need to do in terms of a solution and how you can also maximise the impact and outcomes you achieve for people and society during the crisis, and in the short-term, medium-term and long-term.

The main priority during a crisis is to think about the short-term outcomes that can be delivered. If you get these right it will mean in the medium-term and long-term you will not need to deliver as much because the demand for the type of support people will need after the crisis will not be so high because you will have met their needs in the short-term.

Prioritise

You may have less resources in terms of staff and finances, so you need to prioritise what you deliver. To prioritise your activities identify the most important outcomes that you want to deliver right now. Check in with your ultimate goal and make sure the outcomes you have identified connect to your overarching ultimate goal and purpose.

Get feedback

Think about continually asking for feedback so you can keep adapting through co-designing your activities, and using a lean minimum viable product model to any new activities you are starting. This will avoid spending too much money or resources on activities that may not achieve the desired impact. Focus on measuring short-term outcomes rather than long-term impact because your activities are adapting based on changing needs. If you do not measure, you will not know if you are adapting your activities in the right way.

Adapt

Focus on the short-term – and continually adapt. As we collectively move through a crisis the problems and support people need will change. To start with fear and immediate issues take priority, but as the crisis continues people adjust and adapt and move to needing support with other things.

Think Maslow's hierarchy of needs – most people will have been knocked back to the lower levels of having physiological or safety needs that become the most urgent things to address. But as we adjust and settle in to the new normal, these priorities will be met, and we will move to a need for love and belonging. You need to recognise and follow this transition in terms of what you deliver and the outcomes you are trying to achieve.

Make decisions

It sounds obvious, but in a crisis making decisions can be hard. The fear of making the wrong decision can stop you from making any decision at all. You need to use the impact data you are collecting for decision-making – and ask yourself these types of questions:

- How well is what you are delivering helping?
- What needs to change?
- Are their new needs you have identified?
- Does this new activity align with our purpose?

Your activities will fall in to the following categories:

- Continue: Things you can carry on delivering (covering the pre, during and post-crisis periods)
- Stop: Things you have had to stop delivering permanently (you know these cannot be delivered any longer even post-crisis)
- Pause: Things you have had to stop delivering temporarily (you are aiming to restart these post-crisis)
- Start: New things you have started delivering permanently (during the crisis and post-crisis)
- Start: New things you have started delivering temporarily (just during the crisis)
- Pause: Things you plan to start delivering (post-crisis)

Throughout your decision-making, use your impact data to decide what to stop, start, pause or continue. The crisis may provide you with new delivery models and services that are worth keeping after the crisis. For those activities, it is worth considering if they achieve the outcomes you want better than your pre-lockdown activities.

SECTION FOUR: FURTHER RESOURCES

GLOSSARY

This Social Value Dictionary is available online via **https://makeanimpactcic.co.uk/news/social-value-dictionary/**

Commissioning and procurement: Commissioning is the process of deciding what public services are needed based on priorities, preparing tender documents outlining requirements, undertaking the procurement process and delivery and review of the contract. Procurement is one part of the commissioning process and is focused on finding a suitable supplier and issuing the contract. For more details go to:
 https://www.gmcvo.org.uk/system/files/issues%2019.pdf

To search for contract opportunities please go to the following sites:
Bloom: https://bloom.services/
Supply Change: https://www.supplychange.co.uk/sign-up
Pro-contract: https://procontract.due-north.com/Login
Contracts Finder:
https://www.contractsfinder.service.gov.uk/Search

Community impact: This is the impact the organisation has on the wider community, for example through community regeneration activities.

CSR (Corporate Social Responsibility): This is where a business that operates to maximise its financial profits, donates, provides sponsorship or contributes a proportion of its profits to good causes or charitable activities (in return for positive publicity in most cases).

Economic impact: This is the impact the organisation has on the economy and on the financial resources people have.

Environmental impact: This is the impact the organisation has on the environment (positive and negative).

Impact: Impact refers to the proportion of the outcomes the organisation can claim they are responsible for achieving.

Impact led strategy: An impact led strategy is where an organisation has decided to develop its strategy by being focused on the impact it wants to create, and to put impact/social value at the heart of its organisation and its activities. For more information go to https://makeanimpactcic.co.uk/2019/04/ignore-the-jargon-this-is-what-an-impact-led-strategy-is-and-why-you-need-it/

Impact management: Impact management is about what an organisation does with the information they have obtained through the impact measurement process to continually improve the organisation so they can increase the level of positive impacts and reduce negative impacts.

Impact measurement: Impact measurement is the process of designing systems, consultation with stakeholders, collecting data and measuring the impact you have. For additional resources go to https://www.inspiringimpact.org/

Impact report: This is a report detailing the impact the organisation or a specific project has had, which includes details of the methodology, consultation process, data and analysis.

Indicator: An indicator is the measure/way of knowing something has occurred and been achieved.

Inputs: Inputs are the resources that are required to deliver a particular product, service, activity or project e.g. money, time and equipment.

Intermediary outcomes: These are outcomes that have to happen before another outcome is achieved. For example to gain employment, an individual may need to achieve outcomes of improved confidence, interview skills and motivation first.

Outcomes: Outcomes are the differences or changes that have occurred with the organisation's stakeholders as a result of the delivery of activities and achievement of outputs – including positive, negative, intended and unintended outcomes.

Outputs: Outputs are the results of activities, services or products the organisation has delivered e.g. 20 people trained or 100 advice sessions provided.

Procurement framework: Suppliers go through the procurement process and tender, and the successful suppliers are put on a procurement framework – which means the organisation can buy from the suppliers on the framework over an agreed time period without having to run a full procurement process each time. For more information go to: https://www.trackerintelligence.com/resources/procurem ent-news/what-is-a-public-sector-framework-agreement/

Profit for purpose business: Profit for purpose businesses have a specific purpose embedded in their strategy that benefits people or the planet and use their profits for this purpose.

Profit with purpose business: Profit with purpose means the business profits MORE WITH a purpose, and that's usually a marketing-led purpose with the primary goal of increasing sales and profits. Their purpose isn't always embedded in the business, part of the culture, ethos, or even their overall strategy.

Social enterprise: A social enterprise is a business with a social or environmental purpose. The purpose is usually defined in the social enterprise's governing documents. For further information go to: https://makeanimpactcic.co.uk/2019/01/video-what-is-a-social-enterprise/ and https://makeanimpactcic.co.uk/2018/02/what-is-a-social-enterprise/

Social Impact: Social impact is often used to refer to the change that happens to people, the economy, the community and the environment as a result of our activities or services. But strictly speaking social impact is about the changes that happen to people and economic impact, environmental impact and community impact can be defined separately. The changes can be positive, negative, intended or unintended. They can also be short, medium or long-term changes.

Social procurement or social purchasing: Social procurement (also called social purchasing) is a way for businesses, public sector bodies and Housing Associations to buy more wisely. It helps to generate social value beyond the goods or services they require. It encourages businesses to buy from organisations that will have a wider benefit on people, the environment or the community.

This could mean buying from social enterprises that use their income for positive social or environmental impact. Social procurement involves deciding what kinds of additional value you want suppliers to provide and asking for that as part of the contract.

Social purpose: This is a purpose that has a positive impact on people or the planet that is placed at the heart of the business or organisation.

Social return on investment (SROI): Social Return on Investment (SROI) is a method for identifying, assessing and valuing the impact a particular project, activity, service or organisation has. Typically, it is used where the services are commissioned from the public sector, funded by a grant making body or investor in order to provide a cost-benefit analysis, which is presented as a ratio showing how for every £1 invested £x of benefit (social value) is produced. SROI is a principles based methodology - for further information please go to https://en.wikipedia.org/wiki/Social_return_on_investment and http://www.socialvalueuk.org/

Social Value: Social value describes the wider social, economic and environmental benefits that derive from an organisation's work or from the commissioning of services or the purchasing of goods. Social value is focused on getting more value from the money we spend. It enables us to maximise the positive impact our work and procurement has on local communities, people and the environment. Social values asks the question, 'If £1 is spent on the delivery of services or the purchasing of goods can that same £1 be used to also produce a wider benefit to the community?'

Social Value Act: The full name for this is the Public Services (Social Value) Act 2012, and it is a piece of UK government legislation that came into force in January 2013 that requires public sector bodies to consider social value in their commissioning and procurement processes. From January 2021 Central Government is required to include social value rather than just consider it, and social value will have a minimum score of 10% for tender evaluations, as well as five themes that suppliers will be required to deliver specific outcomes and evidence of achievement. For more information go to: https://www.gov.uk/government/publications/procurement-policy-note-0620-taking-account-of-social-value-in-the-award-of-central-government-contracts

Social value strategy: A social value strategy shows how social value will be included across the activities an organisation delivers and how the organisation will contribute to achieving social value targets and requirements. Usually as a minimum the strategy ensures compliance with the requirements detailed within the Public Services (Social Value) Act 2012, but many organisations choose to deliver more than the minimum social value requirements.

Stakeholders: Stakeholders are people, groups or organisations that your organisation positively or negatively impacts on, or who can impact on your organisation.

Theory of Change: A theory of change is a process for identifying the key changes that occur and the general route that clients/beneficiaries take through the service or activities to the outcomes and ultimate goal. It highlights the typical relationship between the activities, outcomes and ultimate goal. As a theory it is necessary to test whether the assumptions made are correct by gathering data. For more information please go to https://en.wikipedia.org/wiki/Theory_of_change

Ultimate goal: The ultimate goal describes the bigger picture problem the organisation is trying to solve and the long-term impact the organisation wants to have, for example, no poverty.

Endnotes

[i] The Social Value Principles
https://www.socialvalueuk.org/what-is-social-value/the-principles-of-social-value/

[ii] Social Accounting and Audit Principles
https://www.socialauditnetwork.org.uk/getting-started/what-is-social-accounting-and-audit/

[iii] An introductory guide to the Social Value Act
https://www.gov.uk/government/publications/social-value-act-introductory-guide

[iv] Social procurement policy information in Victoria (Australia)
https://www.localgovernment.vic.gov.au/__data/assets/pdf_file/0027/84825/Beyond-Value-for-Money-Social-Procurement-for-Victorian-Local-Government-2nd-edition.pdf and
https://www.buyingfor.vic.gov.au/victorias-social-procurement-framework

[v] Vancouver's Social Procurement criteria and framework
https://vancouver.ca/doing-business/sustainable-procurement.aspx and Calgary's policy
https://www.calgary.ca/cfod/finance/policies/sustainable-environmental-and-ethical-procurement-policy-seepp/sustainable-environmental-and-ethical-procurement-policy-seepp.html

[vi] Details of the Wellbeing of Future Generations Act in Wales
https://www.futuregenerations.wales/about-us/future-generations-act/

[vii] Community Benefits in Procurement in Scotland
https://www.gov.scot/policies/public-sector-procurement/community-benefits-in-procurement/

viii Social Enterprise UK; Procuring for Good (2016) https://www.socialenterprise.org.uk/policy-and-research-reports/procuring-for-good/

ix Social Value in Central Government Procurement – the announcement https://www.gov.uk/government/news/new-measures-to-deliver-value-to-society-through-public-procurement and the Policy Note with additional details and the full guidance https://www.gov.uk/government/publications/procurement-policy-note-0620-taking-account-of-social-value-in-the-award-of-central-government-contracts

x Bolton at Home: Social Value in Procurement Toolkit https://www.boltonathome.org.uk/working-with-our-contractors-suppliers-to-deliver-social-value

xi Sustainable Development Goals https://sustainabledevelopment.un.org/topics/sustainabledevelopmentgoals

xii Theory of Change Software, Better Evaluation (2020) https://www.betterevaluation.org/en/evaluation-options/TOC_software

xiii Big Society Capital Outcomes Matrix - To help identify outcomes and possible indicators (ways to measure the outcome has been achieved) https://www.goodfinance.org.uk/impact-matrix

xiv National TOMs – mainly economic, supply chain and some environmental outcomes https://socialvalueportal.com/national-toms/

xv The New Economics Foundation; National Accounts of Wellbeing: bringing real wealth onto the balance sheet (2009). https://neweconomics.org/uploads/files/2027fb05fed1554aea_uim6vd4c5.pdf and https://www.nationalaccountsofwellbeing.org

xvi Centre for Wellbeing (nef) Measuring wellbeing: A guide for practitioners (2012) provides details of the different components of wellbeing, as well as how to measure wellbeing

along with examples of questions
https://neweconomics.org/2012/07/measuring-wellbeing
xvii SWEMWBS – for wellbeing - this site has a good
explanation of this https://www.corc.uk.net/outcome-
experience-measures/short-warwick-edinburgh-mental-
wellbeing-scale/
xviii Happiness Pulse website Happiness Pulse – for measuring
health and wellbeing https://www.happinesspulse.org
xix What Works Wellbeing - key drivers of wellbeing for your
workplace and staff
https://whatworkswellbeing.org/product/workplace-wellbeing-
questionnaire-methodology/#. The What Works Wellbeing
website has lots of resources, guides and information around
wellbeing www.whatworkswellbeing.org
xx Patient Activation Measure (PAM) Quick Guide
https://www.england.nhs.uk/wp-
content/uploads/2018/04/patient-activation-measure-quick-
guide.pdf
xxi Adult Social Care Outcomes Tool (ASCOT) developed by the
Personal Social Services Research Unit (PSSRU)
https://www.pssru.ac.uk/ascot/
xxii Strengths and Difficulties Questionnaire
https://www.sdqinfo.org/
xxiii Revised Children's Anxiety and Depression Scale
http://www.socialworkerstoolbox.com/revised-childrens-
anxiety-and-depression-scale-and-subscales-rcads/
xxiv SCORE-15 Index of Family Functioning and Change
https://www.aft.org.uk/page/score
xxv Treatment Outcome Profile (TOP)
https://assets.publishing.service.gov.uk/government/uploads/s
ystem/uploads/attachment_data/file/784927/TOP_form_comm
unity_print_version.pdf
xxvi Social Workers Toolbox
http://www.socialworkerstoolbox.com/

xxvii CAFCASS – resources and questionnaires https://www.cafcass.gov.uk/grown-ups/professionals/resources-for-professionals/

xxviii Manual for Measures of Caring Activities and Outcomes for Children and Young People (Carers Trust), Stephen Joseph, Fiona Becker and Saul Becker, 2nd Edition (2012) https://carers.org/downloads/resources-pdfs/young-carer-assessment-tools/manual-for-measures-of-caring-activities-and-outcomes-for-children-and-young-people.pdf

xxix Personal Social Services Survey of Adult Carers in England 2009-2010 – Survey Development Project – Technical Report, Diane Fox, Jacquetta Holder and Ann Netten (2010), PSSRU. https://www.pssru.ac.uk/pub/dp2643_2.pdf

xxx JET – Journey to Employment Framework has lots of questionnaires for addressing barriers to employment and measuring soft skills https://www.thinknpc.org/resource-hub/the-jet-pack-a-guide-to-using-the-journey-to-employment-framework/

xxxi What Works Wellbeing: Volunteer Wellbeing: What works and who benefits? https://whatworkswellbeing.org/resources/volunteer-wellbeing-what-works-and-who-benefits/

xxxii RCPV (Responding to Child Parent Violence) Project led by University of Brighton http://www.rcpv.eu/resources

xxxiii Clinks: Using off the shelf tools to measure change (2014) https://www.clinks.org/publication/using-shelf-tools-measure-change

xxxiv Outcomes Stars www.outcomesstar.org.uk

xxxv Community Cohesion: A report of the independent review team. Chaired by Ted Cantle. Home Office (2001) https://dera.ioe.ac.uk/14146/1/communitycohesionreport.pdf

xxxvi Arts Council Generic Learning Outcomes https://www.artscouncil.org.uk/measuring-outcomes/generic-learning-outcomes#section-1

xxxvii Evaluation Guidance, Heritage Lottery Fund
https://www.heritagefund.org.uk/good-practice-guidance/evaluation-guidance
xxxviii A quick guide to evaluation, Youth Music
https://network.youthmusic.org.uk/evaluation-guidance-intro
for music based projects with children and young people
xxxix Social Impact of Cultural Activities: Measures,
Evaluation, Indicators, Annalisa Cicerchia (2015)
https://www.researchgate.net/publication/280556721_Social_i
mpact_of_cultural_activities_measures_evaluation_indicators
xl The National Lottery Community Fund, Data and Evidence –
link to framework with details of outcomes measures
https://www.tnlcommunityfund.org.uk/funding/funding-guidance/managing-your-funding/data-and-evidence
xli Using Self-Reported Data for Impact Measurement, Impact
Management Project. Customer Experience Questions
https://impactmanagementproject.com/stakeholder/using-self-reported-data-for-impact-measurement/
xlii SDG Tracker - data and progress by country against the
SDGs https://sdg-tracker.org/
xliii Earthbitant SDG Calculator to track your action and
progress against specific goals https://www.earthbitant.com/
xliv SDG Impact Assessment Tool – a self assessment tool to
identify your contribution to the SDGs
https://sdgimpactassessmenttool.org
xlv SDG Compass – lists a range of tools that can be used for
specific goals https://sdgcompass.org/business-tools/
xlvi Pro-environmental behaviour scales – for measuring
changes in behaviour around the environment. Measuring
pro-environmental behaviour – review and recommendations,
Journal of Environmental Psychology (2019), Florian Lange
and Siegfried Dewitte.
https://www.researchgate.net/publication/332678043_Measuri
ng_pro-environmental_behavior_Review_and_recommendations

[xlvii] CoGo Carbon Footprint tracker https://cogo.co/

[xlviii] thredUP Fashion Footprint Calculator https://www.thredup.com/fashionfootprint

[xlix] Supply Chain School https://www.supplychainschool.co.uk

[l] Asket: The Impact Receipt https://www.asket.com/transparency/impact

[li] Nef Consulting Environmental Indicators https://www.nefconsulting.com/our-services/evaluation-impact-assessment/prove-and-improve-toolkits/environmental-indicators/

[lii] Carbon figures for different farming methods: http://www.coolfarmtool.org/, https://www.agrecalc.com/ and https://farmcarbontoolkit.org.uk/carbon-calculator

[liii] Carbon figures for different travel methods: https://www.carbonfootprint.com/calculator.aspx

[liv] Carbon figures for different food choices: https://meals4planet.org/calculator/

[lv] Why data centres are the new frontier in the fight against climate change, Charlotte Trueman, Computer World (August 2019) https://www.computerworld.com/article/3431148/why-data-centres-are-the-new-frontier-in-the-fight-against-climate-change.html

[lvi] The Carbon footprint of 'thank you' emails, Martin Armstrong (December 2019) https://www.statista.com/chart/20189/the-carbon-footprint-of-thank-you-emails/#:~:text=The%20sending%20of%20one%20email,at%20on%20a%20national%20scale

[lvii] WebCarbon Calculator for digital footprint (developed by Petr Kirpeit and Digital Harz). https://co2.digitaler-harz.de/

[lviii] Ecosia – the search engine that plants trees https://www.ecosia.org

[lix] Tab for a Cause https://tab.gladly.io/

[lx] Cleanfox https://www.cleanfox.io/

[lxi] Greengeeks green webhosting https://www.greengeeks.com/

lxii Kualo green webhosting
https://www.kualo.co.uk/webhosting/green-web-hosting
lxiii Survey Builder Tools:
Survey Monkey https://www.surveymonkey.com
FreeOnlineSurveys https://www.freeonlinesurveys.com
YesInsights https://www.yesinsights.com
QuickTapSurvey https://www.quicktapsurvey.com
Survey Anyplace https://www.surveyanyplace.com
Surveybot https://www.surveybot.io
SmartSurvey https://www.smartsurvey.co.uk
lxiv Form Builder Apps:
Google Forms https://docs.google.com/forms
Typeform https://www.typeform.com
Microsoft Forms https://forms.microsoft.com
Wufoo https://www.wufoo.com
JotForm https://www.jotform.com
lxv Zapier – https://www.zapier.com
lxvi Online polls and live audience feedback apps:
Mentimeter https://www.mentimeter.com
Poll Junkie https://www.polljunkie.com
Easy Polls https://www.easypolls.net
Poll Everywhere https://www.polleverywhere.com
lxvii Online Interactive Whiteboards:
Google Jamboard https://jamboard.google.com
Miro https://www.miro.com
Ideaboardz https://www.ideaboardz.com
lxviii Survey Monkey's Sample Size Calculator:
https://www.surveymonkey.com/mp/sample-size-calculator/
lxix Sources of financial values/proxies includes: New Economy
Manchester Unit Cost Database
https://www.greatermanchester-ca.gov.uk/what-we-
do/research/research-cost-benefit-analysis/; NHS Reference
Costs https://www.gov.uk/government/publications/nhs-
reference-costs-2015-to-2016 (then select the National
schedule of reference costs: main schedule which is an excel

spreadsheet); PSSRU Unit costs of Health and Social Care https://www.pssru.ac.uk/project-pages/unit-costs/unit-costs-2018/ (You can then either download the complete document or sections); Global Value Exchange (database to search for financial values) www.globalvaluexchange.org and HACT Value calculator (mainly for housing related projects but worth looking at if you can't find a value elsewhere) http://www.hact.org.uk/value-calculator

lxx The Value Game http://www.valuegame-online.org/

lxxi This figure is taken from the New Economy Manchester Unit Cost Database V2.0 https://www.greatermanchester-ca.gov.uk/what-we-do/research/research-cost-benefit-analysis/

lxxii The Value Game http://www.valuegame-online.org/

lxxiii Social Value UK https://www.socialvalueuk.org/

lxxiv Social Value International https://socialvalueint.org/

lxxv The GIIN: The Business Value of Impact Measurement (2016) https://thegiin.org/assets/GIIN_ImpactMeasurementReport_webfile.pdf

lxxvi Balanced Scorecard, Robert S. Kaplan and David P. Norton, (1992) https://en.wikipedia.org/wiki/Balanced_scorecard

lxxvii Examples of Impact Reports:
Innovating Minds: http://www.ypacademy.org.uk/wp-content/uploads/2018/03/IM-Social-Impact-Report-2018.pdf
whg https://www.whg.uk.com/wp-content/uploads/2020/09/whg-social-value-report-2019-min.pdf
Provide CIC https://www.provide.org.uk/modules/downloads/download.php?file_name=232
Central England Co-op https://www.centralengland.coop/assets/documents/Social_Impact_report.pdf
Pennine Lancashire Community Farm – Video Impact Report https://www.penninelancashirecommunityfarm.org/social-impact-report-2018/

AgilityEco – Infographic Impact Report using the SDGs
https://www.agilityeco.co.uk/news/agilityeco-presents-its-social-and-environmental-impact-2018
lxxviii Canva – for designing infographics, social media posts and brochures/reports https://www.canva.com
lxxix For creating videos from text and images https://lumen5.com/
lxxx Animated video creation https://www.powtoon.com/
lxxxi 10 infographic examples https://www.classy.org/blog/10-nonprofit-infographics-inspire-inform
lxxxii Thinglink – for interactive images https://www.thinglink.com
lxxxiii SDG Impact Standards https://sdgimpact.undp.org/
lxxxiv Impact Management Project https://impactmanagementproject.com/
lxxxv Global Reporting Initiative Standards https://www.globalreporting.org/standards/
lxxxvi Doughnut Economics: 7 ways to think like a 21st century economist, Kate Raworth (2017) and the Doughnut Economics Action Lab https://doughnuteconomics.org/

Free Resources

These are available for you to download for free.

To get your free resources go to https:///www.makeanimpactcic.co.uk/impact-first-resources

Includes:

- Theory of Change Worksheet
- Impact Measurement Framework
- Social Value Checklist
- Organisation Self-assessment questionnaire
- Board Self-assessment questionnaire
- Links to blogs and podcasts on IMM

Additional guidance and freebies added regularly!

Impact Diaries Podcast

For examples and further guidance listen to the Impact Diaries Podcast – eight episodes covering the five stages of the lean social impact approach, the cross cutting themes, economic, environmental & tech impact and social procurement. https://makeanimpactcic.co.uk/news/make-an-impact-podcast/make-an-impact-podcast-pt2

Theory of Change Worksheet

Inputs (the resources that are needed to deliver the activities)	
Activities (the activities, products or services you deliver)	
Outputs (the numbers of the activities/people) e.g. 20 sessions delivered	
Outcomes (the intermediate changes that have to happen to achieve your long-term impact)	
Long-term impact (your ultimate goal and the long-term changes you want to achieve)	

Download from https://www.makeanimpactcic.co.uk/impact-first-resources

Impact Measurement Framework

Stakeholder	Example: Young people
What key outcomes do you want to measure?	Ability to sustain employment
Data currently collected	Anecdotal via session records
What indicator/measure will you use? (the way of knowing the outcome is achieved)	Statement: I have the support and help I need to stay in work
How and when collected	Self assessed using scale strongly agree-strongly disagree. Collected at 1st session on registration form and 3 months later on review form.

Download from https://www.makeanimpactcic.co.uk/impact-first-resources

Social Value Checklist

Complete this checklist and see where you are in terms of developing your social impact measurement, management and reporting process.

Download from
https://www.makeanimpactcic.co.uk/impact-first-resources

Question	Yes/No	Comments and additional information
1. Do you have a clearly defined purpose that includes how you benefit people or the planet?		
2. Does your strategy link to the impact you want to have?		
3. Do you link your activities to your purpose?		
4. Can you describe the positive outcomes you want to achieve?		
5. Do you know who your stakeholders are?		
6. Do you know the impact you have on your stakeholders?		

7. Do you engage and consult with your stakeholders?		
8. Do you know what outcomes are important to each of your stakeholders? 9. Do you collect data on these?		
10. Do you collect feedback on your activities?		
11. Do you collect data on the outcomes you achieve?		
12. Do you understand how your activities link to your outcomes?		
13. Do you have a theory of change developed?		
14. Do you regularly review and update your theory of change?		
15. Do you have KPIs and performance measures for impact?		
16. Do you link your impact measurement to continuous improvement within your organisation?		

17. Do you have any of the following forms of feedback and data:		
Questionnaires/surveys		
Interviews		
Focus groups		
Case studies		
Project evaluations		
Reports for funders		
Videos		
18. Do you regularly consult with the following via a questionnaire:		
Beneficiaries/clients		
Staff		
Volunteers		
Board members		
Partner organisations		
Funders		
Wider community		

19. Do you report your impact via the following:		
A separate social, economic and environmental impact report		
Through your annual report/accounts		
Verbally at trustee/board meetings		
Newsletters		
Case studies		
Internal reports for management/the board		
Evaluations for funders		
KPIs and targets for impact		
20. Do you regularly talk about your impact via:		
Agenda items at Board meetings		
Discussions with staff		

Discussions with stakeholders		
Discussions with the wider community		
21. Do you use any automated systems to:		
Collect data		
Analyse data		
Produce reports		
22. Why do you want to measure your social impact? Please rank your responses in order of priority (with 1 being the highest priority and 7 the lowest):		
To report back to a funder		
To communicate what we do and our impact		
To make sure we are operating effectively		
To identify where we can make improvements		
To evidence how we comply with the Social Value Act		
To identify the potential savings we make for the public sector		
To monetise our social value and calculate a SROI figure		

23. What is your capacity internally to undertake impact measurement? **Please state Yes/No**	
We have limited resources (time, money and staff) and are new to impact measurement	
We are experienced in using impact measurement systems	
We are committed to measuring our impact but staff have little time to implement this	
We have lots of data but currently don't do anything with it and need help to establish systems and ways to analyse this data	
24. What are you interested in measuring? **Please state Yes/No**	
Our social impact	
Our environmental impact	
Our economic impact	
All three (social, economic and environmental impact)	
A specific project/area of our work	

Organisation Self-assessment questionnaire: Social Impact Measurement and Management

Complete this self-assessment to see how you score for implementation of IMM in your organisation.

Download from https://www.makeanimpactcic.co.uk/impact-first-resources

Question	Low	Medium	High
Overall purpose			
Do you have a clear objective or purpose for your social impact work?	No	It is led by funders' evaluation requirements and evidencing success for them	Yes it is about proving or improving – and we are really clear which one it is.
Is there a focus for your social impact measurement?	No – we are doing a bit of everything and not really doing any of it very well	For some projects or services we are really focused and clear, but for others we aren't	For all projects and services we are really clear

Current awareness of impact			
Do you know what impact your work has?	No – we only have some anecdotal feedback	For some areas of our work we know what difference it makes	For all areas of our work we are very clear about the impact it has
Do you know about any unexpected changes/ or negative outcomes you create?	No – we focus on the positive outcomes only	We are aware of these but don't do anything to investigate further	Yes we use this information to continually improve our services
Have you got a clear theory of change?	No	For some areas of work	Yes for all our work
Do you know which activities contribute most to your impact? And which don't add much value?	No – we treat all our activities the same	We think some activities achieve more than others but don't have much data to support this	We know exactly which activities deliver the most impact and have a plan to focus on doing more of these

Involvement of leadership			
Do you have decision makers supporting the process of impact measurement?	No	There is some support for impact measurement, but operational stuff usually gets in the way	Yes there are senior management and Board members involved in developing this
Is impact measurement one person's responsibility?	Yes	It is mostly one person with some support from a few others	No – it's shared across a number of job roles
Do you need more leadership from the Board on impact measurement?	Yes – they are currently not involved	Sometimes – they don't always see the importance of impact measurement or why we are bothering	No – they fully support impact measurement

On-going process/culture of continuous improvement			
Is your impact reporting a one off?	Yes – we have no plans to make it an on-going process	Partly – some areas we are developing on-going systems	No – it's part of our on-going systems and processes
Have you thought about how to report back to different stakeholders?	No	We have some different communic-ations but we are not sure they are appropriate	Yes – we communic-ate in a range of ways to get the key messages across to different stakeholder-rs
Do you know how your organisation compares to other organisations providing similar services?	No	We have some information – but it's only for some areas of our work	Yes – we benchmark our performanc e and use this to see where we can improve
Do you know how you could	No	We could probably deliver our services in	Yes – we have identified areas

increase your impact?		better ways but we're not really sure	where outcomes and impact is lower than others, and are working to improve these
Does impact measurement drive learning and improvement?	No	Sometimes changes are made following the impact measurem-ent and feedback	Yes – we identify areas for learning and improvem-ent each time we analyse the data
Embedding impact			
Is impact measurement incorporated at each level of your charity: **Strategy Business planning and development Board discussions HR appraisals and objectives**	No – none of these areas	In some of these areas – for example, we use it sometimes when business planning	Yes – we have a clear plan to integrate impact measurem-ent in all aspects of the organisati-on, so we are impact led in our

Finance Service quality and improvement Performance measurement			decision making and processes

Board Self-assessment questionnaire: Social impact measurement

Use this self-assessment to assess your Board and their knowledge, usage and involvement in IMM.

Download from https://www.makeanimpactcic.co.uk/impact-first-resources

Question	Low	Medium	High
The Board know what social impact measurement is	No	Some understanding	Clear understanding
There are people on the Board with expertise and knowledge in social impact measurement	No	1 or 2 have some experience	Yes – we have several individuals with expertise
The Board consider impact measurement important to the success of the organisation	No	Sometimes	Yes
The Board assume the work has a positive impact as the organisation does good work in	Yes	Frequently	No

the community – so measuring impact is not a priority			
The Board agree outcome based metrics and goals with staff as well as activity/efficiency measures for 1-3 years	No	Occasionally – usually for specific projects or activities	Yes – time is dedicated to this annually
The Board regularly monitor and discuss the impact of the organisation	No	Sometimes – typically when there are issues with delivery	Yes
Leadership require impact measurement data on projects/services	No	Sometimes	Always
The Board uses feedback from stakeholders to inform strategy and resource allocation	No	Partially	Always
The charity's strategy is based	No	Sometimes – but this is usually by	Yes – we focus on delivering activities that

on maximising impact		accident rather than strategically decided	generate the most impact
When discussing options/future activities the impact is routinely discussed to help make decisions	No	Sometimes	Yes – it is a vital component of decision making
As part of the senior management teams' appraisals the Board include objectives around impact	No	Occasionally	Always
Financial decisions also include measures for impact	No	Sometimes	Usually
Achieving continuous improvement and increasing impact are important to the Board	No	Occasionally	Always

INDEX

ABOUT THE AUTHOR

Heidi Fisher MBE is a multi-award winning specialist in social enterprise and social impact. She received an MBE for Services to Innovation in Social Enterprise and to Impact Measurement in the 2020 New Year Honours.

Heidi's background is as a Chartered Accountant, having set up the UK's first social enterprise Chartered Accountancy firm in 2008. Heidi first started working in impact measurement in 2002, and trained in Social Accounting and Social Return on Investment. Heidi has worked with over 2,100 social enterprises, from start-ups to those with over £1billion of income, supporting them to become more sustainable, develop their trading income and to better measure, manage and communicate their impact. As well as this book, Heidi is the author of the best-selling book, "Social Enterprise: How to successfully set up and grow a social enterprise."

Her vision is a world where all businesses are social enterprises that positively impact people and the planet. Heidi is passionate about leaving a positive legacy for her children and society.

Get in touch with Heidi:

W: https://www.makeanimpactcic

T: https://www.twitter.com/heidilfisher

L: https://www.linkedin.com/in/heidilfisher

I: https://www.instagram.com/heidi.fisher

F: Join Heidi's Facebook Group: Social Enterprise Success
https://www.facebook.com/groups/socialenterprisesuccess

Get your free resources:
https://www.makeanimpactcic.co.uk/impact-first-resources

Printed in Great Britain
by Amazon

58450611R00129